Todd + Mo

May your a... filled with TONS rainbow moments!

Rainbows and Banana Peels

Katharine C [illegible]

OTHER BOOKS BY KATHARINE C. GIOVANNI

Going Above and Beyond

The Concierge Manual

The Concierge Manual Workbook

God, Is That You?

101 Great Ways to Improve Your Life: Volume 3
(Contributing Author)

Inspiring Hope
(Contributing Author)

Rainbows and Banana Peels

Surviving Life's Knocks with Grace

Katharine C. Giovanni

NewRoad Publishing
Wake Forest, North Carolina

RAINBOWS AND BANANA PEELS

Published by:
NewRoad Publishing
3650 Rogers Road, #328, Wake Forest, NC 27587
Telephone: 919-443-2425
E-mail: Ron@NewRoadPublishing.com

An application to register this book for cataloging has been submitted to the Library of Congress.

First Edition

ISBN: 978-1-931109-04-8

Printed in the United States of America

Editing and Layout by Sherry Roberts, The Roberts Group
Cover design by Harmonie Ponder, Ponder Consulting
Cover photograph by Nancy Jones Photography

Disclaimers and Legal Notices

The information presented herein is not presented with the intention of diagnosing or treating any disease or condition. For diagnosis or treatment of any medical problem, consult your own physician. The information presented herein is for educational purposes and should not be interpreted as medical advice. No responsibility is assumed by the author nor anyone connected with this book for the use of this information and no guarantees of any kind are made for the performance or effectiveness of the recommendations provided. The publisher and author are not responsible for any specific health or allergy needs that may require medical supervision and are not liable for any damages or negative consequences from any treatment, action, application or preparation, to any person reading or following the information in this book.

Information Accuracy

The author and NewRoad Publishing make every effort to ensure that all information presented in this book is correct. However, we do not guarantee the accuracy of the information contained in this book, and reliance on information provided in this book is solely at your own risk. Every effort has been made to make this book as complete as possible; however, it may yet contain mistakes, both typographical and substantive. Therefore, this book should be used only as a general guide and not as the ultimate source of information on the concierge industry.

Disclaimer of Warranties

This book is provided solely on an "as-is" basis, and the use of the information contained herein is at your sole risk. Except to the extent required by any mandatory applicable law, this book and the information contained herein are not subject to any warranty or condition, express or implied, including, without limitation, any warranty of merchantability, satisfactory quality, fitness for a particular purpose or use, or non-infringement.

Neither the author nor NewRoad Publishing guarantees the accuracy or completeness of any information contained in this book. Neither the author nor NewRoad Publishing assumes any liability or responsibility for any errors or omissions in the information contained in the book. Neither the author nor NewRoad Publishing makes any representations or warranties of any kind, express or implied, as to the book or the information contained herein or the results that may be obtained from the use of information contained in the book.

Limitation of Liability

Neither the author nor NewRoad Publishing shall be liable for any damages of any kind arising from or in connection with the use of the book or the information contained therein, including, without limitation, mistakes, omissions, errors, or defects, even if the author or NewRoad Publishing is expressly advised of the possibility of such damages. This is a comprehensive limitation of liability that applies to all damages of any kind, including compensatory, direct, indirect, punitive, special, incidental, or consequential damages (including but not limited to damages for lost profits or loss of revenue).

You haven't reached the end;
you have reached the beginning of a brand new journey.
See that door ahead?
It just opened for you.
Your new life starts right now.

KATHARINE C. GIOVANNI

For My Family

CONTENTS

INTRODUCTION

MY LIFE HAS BEEN A series of high peaks and extremely dark valleys. I have lived in heaven and have wallowed in the depths of hell.

Yet I am still here.

More to the point, my life has been a life of beautiful rainbows and extremely slippery banana peels.

In fact, I've often found myself in a field of banana peels. Now there's a rough place to get out of. The minute you get back on your feet—WHAM! You slip on another peel and back down you go. The trick is to not let the circumstances that landed you in that darn field get into the core of your being.

The bad news is that the entrance to the field disappears the minute you walk in. You can't go back. The good news is that the exit is on the other side of the field.

The key is to rise above it and keep your eye on the edge of the field because that's the way out. On hands and knees . . . one step at a time . . . I've crawled my way out of the insanity of the banana peel fields.

NO ONE is the same person when they get out. You are different. Your life is different.

So you escape the field and are high on a rainbow for a while. How spectacular! Your life is going smoothly, you're in a great relationship, you have money, life is good and then . . .

Wait for it . . .

WHAM.

Back down you go.

What happened?

Rainbows are *slippery*! It takes *work* to stay on top of them. Be careful because when you slide off the rainbow, banana peels instantly appear all around you, and you often don't see them until you are flat on your back.

Again.

Sigh.

I've been there and done that a bunch of times. So many times you would think that I am pretty good at staying out of those particular fields.

Wrong.

Life has a way of hitting you from behind when you are not looking, and quite often it will knock you flat. As I said, the trick is to not stay there. You have to get up again. Don't allow your circumstances to slip into your soul because, if you do, it's really hard to get out of the banana peel field.

If you want to stay on the rainbow, then you have to believe that you can and think positively. Consistent negative thoughts such as "I'll always be fat" or "I'll never have enough money" will keep you in the banana peel fields.

That being said, the only real way I can help you out of your banana peel field is to walk you through some of mine. Some were easy to get out of; others were hell—but I always get out. I am a fighter who wins her battles.

At the end of the day, we come into this world alone and we leave alone, and along the way, we make decisions on how we want our life to play out. Some work, others don't. Some raise us up on the rainbow, and others plunge us into the banana peel fields. The trick to life is to learn from your stay in the fields and try and stay on the rainbows for as long as possible.

That's life, though, isn't it? Life is filled with breathtaking rainbow moments and interminable journeys through the banana peel fields.

My biggest banana peel? Stage 3 breast cancer in 2012 at the age of fifty-one.

So how did I get through all these negative events in my life and still remain positive? Wasn't always easy. Often it was a minute-by-minute choice.

Being positive is a lifestyle choice.

It's a way of life that you choose.

This book is going to show you the tools that I used to get out of the banana peel fields and back up on that wonderful, beautiful, and quite slippery rainbow. Sometimes I had help getting out; other times I had to pull myself out.

You're going to discover that this is a *really* different type of book. Is this a self-help book? Absolutely, who else will do it for you? Is it a memoir? Yep, it's that, too. You're going to read about some of my banana peel fields.

So which is it?

Actually, it's two books in one designed to help you figure out how to get out of your banana peel field. I'm here to show you the way.

So buckle up your seat belt. Your old self is now a memory, and your new life starts right now.

> KEY TO THIS BOOK: The memoir chapters in this book are denoted with a banana peel. (After all, I spend a lot of time remembering my days in the banana peel fields in those chapters.) The self-help chapters, which have great tips, are denoted with a rainbow because I hope they help you stay on your rainbow.

CHAPTER ONE

What Happens When God Throws a Book at You

IT WAS A DARK AND stormy night.

No, that's not right, I thought to myself. You can't start a book like this by quoting Snoopy.

As I sat at my desk, I looked out the window. It was a beautiful sunny day. I stared at the blue sky and thought back to everything that had happened to me since that fateful day so many years ago. It certainly has been a wild ride. Being a writer, I have never had trouble writing before, but this book was different, and quite frankly, I didn't know where to start.

With nothing coming to mind, I finally gave up.

Perhaps a cup of tea will inspire me, I thought to myself, rising from my desk.

As I walked into the kitchen, my mind spun back to that fateful Wednesday when it all began and my world turned upside down.

It was the fall of 1996. I woke up like I always did and immediately headed for the coffee. I poured myself a cup from the pot, walked into our little family room, and sat on the couch. It was actually quite peaceful sitting there listening to the silence of the apartment. At least it was until my husband and two little boys woke up. The peace of the morning shattered into a million pieces as the boys ran into my arms talking a mile a minute.

A few hours later, with my husband off to work, I settled my sons in front of the television so they could watch an episode of *Barney*. I lovingly patted each one on the top of the head and turned to go back into the kitchen.

As I rounded the corner, I saw someone standing in the kitchen hall. My heart immediately leaped into my throat as I opened my mouth to scream. Before any sound could come out of my mouth, however, the woman smiled at me and vanished.

I rubbed my eyes and looked again.

Nothing.

I'm crazy, I thought, now I'm starting to see things. I really need to get more sleep. Too many sleepless nights with two restless toddlers were starting to get to me.

So I did what I always did when things I couldn't explain happened to me. I ignored the entire episode.

As I went through the day, I couldn't get the woman out of my mind. I remembered that she was very beautiful and wore a long brocade dress with ribbons running down the front. The fact that I could see right through her wasn't lost on me.

For the next two weeks I tried my best to forget what I saw, but questions kept creeping back into my mind.

Was the woman an angel? Did they exist? Was I crazy?

Should I be on medication of some sort?

I had no answers and no one to ask as we were new in town and hadn't met many people yet. Eventually, I told my husband, who just looked at me like I was nuts.

"You saw what?"

"I'm telling you, I think I saw an angel standing in the kitchen hall."

"You're crazy," he said. "It's just your mind playing tricks on you. Stress does that."

"I know what I saw!"

To which he just stared at me. To be honest, he actually looked like he was mentally trying to figure out what size straight jacket would fit me.

At that point, one of the boys started to cry, so the conversation was tabled for another day.

The following morning I still couldn't get the angel out of my mind. She *was* an angel right? What else could it have been?

Although I wasn't a particularly religious person, something had clearly happened to me. So shouldn't I do something? Perhaps I should start thanking God for things, I thought. Maybe I should start going to church again, I wondered out loud to the empty room. Well, at the very least I can start praying and saying thank you for things.

At least it's a start, right?

So after breakfast, I silently thanked God for the meal, and then immediately heard the words, "You're welcome," form in my mind.

Huh?

Now that was an odd. Why would I think the words "You're welcome"? I wondered.

At this point, I was seriously considering going to a doctor and asking for some type of medication. Was I going mad? Lack of sleep, stress, maybe it was all just catching up to me.

As the day went on, I continued to thank God for various things, and each and every time I did, I would hear myself think the words, "You're welcome."

Okay, that's it, I thought. I'm clearly sick. First, I'm seeing things, then I'm talking to myself, and now I'm hearing things. Funny, I didn't *feel* sick. In fact, I felt perfectly fine.

Although I hadn't had a drink in years, I probably would have had one if it had been handy. Luckily for me, it wasn't. So I did what every reasonable person would do. I went to the bookstore to see if someone had written a book on this (we didn't have access to the Internet in that apartment). I had no idea what I was looking for but didn't know what else to do. I didn't really want to tell anybody about my experience because I was scared they would think I was schizophrenic or something. Only crazy people hear voices in their head, right?

Later that afternoon when my sons were playing a game with their father, I drove to the local bookstore.

Since I had no idea what I was looking for, I randomly picked an aisle to walk down and looked at the books. As I rounded the fifth aisle, a book flew off the shelf at me.

Startled and more than a little curious, especially since books generally don't throw themselves at me, I walked around to the other side to see who had knocked the book off the shelf—only to find that no one was there. So I went back and picked up the book and read the title. Amazingly, it was *Conversations with God* by Neale Donald Walsch.

It was in that very instant that I realized "who" had been saying, "You're welcome" to me for the last few days.

It was God!

Oh my God! I thought ironically.

Since God was now throwing things at me to *get* my attention, I decided that perhaps it was time to start *paying* attention.

My hands immediately started to shake as I flipped through the pages of the book. I just couldn't believe that God had the time to talk to me.

Why would He talk to me? I wondered. I'm not anyone important; just a normal person trying to make it through the day as best as I could. I'm not even religious! So why would He talk to me?

Since I didn't need God to throw any more books at me, or worse, I quickly went to the cashier and raced back to my car.

For the next few days, I did nothing but read. I was like a woman possessed and tore through the pages like a rocket. After I finished, I laid the book on the table and sat back.

Not really expecting an answer, I decided to try and start up a conversation.

What have I got to lose? I thought.

"God, are you still there?" I meekly asked out loud to the empty room.

"Yes. I'm here. Where else would I be?" I heard Him reply again in my head.

My heart skipped a beat; I couldn't believe it.

Perhaps I should ask something, I thought. Since I was still considering going back to church, I decided that it was a logical place to start.

"I'm thinking of going back to church and am wondering if I should choose something besides Episcopalian. I mean, what religion is the right religion to choose? There are so many," I asked out loud to the empty room.

"Just follow me," God replied.

Which is exactly what I've been doing ever since.

What I didn't know then was that my life's course had just changed, and I had just left the starting gate.

I snapped myself back from the past, made myself a hot cup of tea, and returned to my office.

About an hour later, I was sitting at my computer again staring at the empty page in front of me.

So how exactly do you start a book like this, I silently wondered. How do you write a book about staying positive while the world is throwing things at your head? Breast cancer, business failures, business successes, family drama—I have lived through it all.

I didn't do it alone, though, I thought to myself smiling.

With nothing in mind, and no direction to follow, I started typing.

CHAPTER TWO

Are You Happy Yet?

HAPPINESS.

That's the destination, right?

We are all desperately seeking happiness.

So let me ask you a question: Are you happy?

I know many people who are happy, but they tell me that they try to downplay it so as not to upset anyone.

Can you imagine? Hiding the fact that you are actually happy?

Really?

How are you? people ask.

Oh, I'm hanging in there, they automatically reply.

Then there are the people who greet you with a "Hello, how are you?" Americans don't want you to reply, though. It's merely a greeting. No one cares.

I'm a bit different because if you ask me this question, I will actually answer the question.

"I'm hungry actually." "I'm fabulous."

Here's how I usually answer: "I'm happy; how are you?"

You should see the looks I get.

Let's pretend I'm the genie in the bottle, and I have the power to make you happy.

So back to my original question: Are you happy?

Well, you reply, I'm sick and don't feel well. I would like to be healthy again. That will make me happy.

I do my genie thing. BAM! You are now healthy. Are you happy now?

Well, not exactly, you reply. I can't be happy because I have too many bills to pay. I also have this, that, and the next thing.

Okay, I'll keep playing. What would make you happy now?

Money, you reply. I would be happy if I had enough money.

BAM! You have won the lottery, and *all* your bills are paid. You have a stunning new house, and your life has all the bells and whistles that you can possibly imagine. Certainly, you are happy now.

No, I'm not because now this and that has happened, but I can be happy if you give me . . .

What is going on?

Your life has certainly changed, but the reality is that although you have moved beyond your old circumstances, your new life has come with its own set of unique problems and circumstances. So your happiness gets pushed to the back, while you deal with the new "stuff" that has come into your life.

When are you going to be happy? Next year? In ten years? When you're ninety-five years old?

Now, I'm not suggesting by any means that you should ignore the challenging times in which we live. I'm simply encouraging you to go out into the world with a healthy positive attitude. I'm encouraging you to be a lighthouse for people. Show the world how to do it right by being the *example.*

Here's a *really* crazy thought:

Be willing to give up difficulty so that you can be a shining example of what humanity can be!

Be willing to be happy!

Sound crazy? Sound outrageous? Sound possible?

Now don't get me wrong here. I have certainly had my ups and downs. I have fallen down thousands of times, and I have made hundreds of mistakes. Yet, incredibly, I am still here. The trick to creating a successful life is to get back up after you fall.

Listen, you are going to make mistakes; things are going to happen; things are going to go wrong. That's part of life. The important thing to remember is how you greet these things when they happen. It's your perspective of the events that will make or break you. Do you stay down on the floor in the fetal position, or do you get up and try again?

According to Shawn Achor, author of the incredible book *The Happiness Advantage*, studies show that only 10 percent of your happiness comes from outside sources. That means that 90 percent of your happiness is actually an inside job. It comes from deep within you.

Would it also surprise you that, according to a study conducted by Albert Mehrabian, it was found that 58 percent of your message is conveyed through body language, 38 percent by tone of voice, and only 7 percent by the actual words spoken?

So that means that whatever is in your 90 percent, whether positive or negative, will *bleed* through your body language. People will *see* that you are unhappy whether you want them to or not.

It will also directly affect your health. If 90 percent of your body is unhappy and angry, how do you think that will affect your health? Anger is toxic.

So, exactly how do you be happy in today's challenging world?

Believe it or not, there are actually people who are living a happy life and are enjoying it. They're not very loud and vocal about it, but they're there.

Isn't it time you were one of them?

CHAPTER THREE

The Banana Peel Fields: Watch Where You Step

I LEANED BACK AND STARED at the computer screen.

Being happy and staying positive, I thought to myself, is *not* always easy. Life is hard. Plus, it's hard to be positive when things are hitting the fan all the time

I need some air, I thought to myself.

I walked downstairs, tugged on my shoes, and went outside.

It didn't help, though. As much as I tried, I couldn't get my mind off the book I was writing. I tried to banish memories of my youth from my mind, but I couldn't.

As I walked, I could feel the cold brushing my shoulders. Although it was a beautiful day, I wasn't paying attention to it. My mind kept wandering to the past. It was as if ancient ghosts were following me down the road purposely pushing my mind further and further back to the past.

After a while, I stopped fighting them. The minute I did, they grabbed me by the shoulders and gently tossed me back to a time long ago.

I am a positive person. Always have been. It's in my nature to look at the silver linings of dark things and to be the one in the group spurring people on.

When I was a little girl, we had a summer house on the Jersey shore. Although I have no memory of it, my father often told me that I would ride my pink bicycle with fat white tires up and down the block saying hello to everyone I met. He said I was like a little ball of love. I couldn't have been more than five or six. Years later, during my dark teenage years, my father would often ask me where that little girl went.

It was a good question. Where did that loving little girl go? It took a long time, but I eventually found her again when I hit my late thirties.

You see, for most of my childhood, it often felt like I was in one large banana peel field. The minute I figured out how to stand up, someone would knock me back down again.

I was born in 1961 and was raised in New York City by an emotionally poor family. I was bullied in elementary school and went home each night to a perfectly dysfunctional alcoholic family, where I was frequently ignored. I was shy by nature so being ignored all the time only made it worse. Since I didn't want anyone to find out how bad it was at home, I learned to stuff my emotions deep inside of me and put on a brave face whenever I left the house.

I have always loved to read and write, and as a child, I learned that books were the key to my survival. So every day, I would flee to a world where families actually loved each other and people were happy—the world of make-believe. I devoured books such as *Little House on the Prairie,* reading them over and over again. Laura Ingalls Wilder had the family that I yearned for, and at least for a while when I was reading, I could pretend that her family was my own. Every day I would step into a rainbow world where Laura's family would welcome me with warmth, love, friendship, and open arms. The imaginary world of books was safer and a lot more fun than my house, so I lost myself in them and took a daily vacation from my problems.

Some days I would flee to my friend Vivienne's house, and we would talk for hours about what we would be when we grew up. I was invited to stay for dinner at Viv's house a lot, and her parents (who were both doctors) would ask me about my day, give me advice about school, make me do my homework, and offer solutions on how to deal with the bullies who hassled me. Viv would talk about becoming a doctor (she is an extremely successful vascular surgeon today), and I would daydream about helping people. I had no idea what I wanted to do exactly, but I knew I wanted to make a difference.

Often in his drunken stupor, my father would tell me that I would never amount to anything so I might as well just get married and have children. That one comment stayed with me for years, although not in the way you might think. In a strange way, my father actually did me a favor. Telling me I can't do something has always been a serious motivator for me. His words actually encouraged me to do the exact opposite, if only to prove him wrong.

It was a dark childhood that forced me to grow up much too soon.

My father achieved sobriety sooner than my mother did. Once he became sober, he divorced my mother and moved out of the city to start a new life with a new family. Since my brother was in boarding school, and my father's new wife didn't like me, I was left alone with my alcoholic mother.

Now don't get me wrong, my mother was a loving person, but she was also an absolutely horrible drunk. Her personality did a 180-degree turn when she drank. She became critical, sarcastic, angry, and possessive. When sober, she was warm, friendly, and loving.

I remember those days as being among the hardest of my youth as I constantly tried to get my mother sober. I hid bottles, I yelled, I screamed, I cajoled, and I even marked her bottles to see how much she was actually drinking. Nothing worked. So in 1977, I simply left my entire family behind and went to boarding school. I didn't need these crazy people, I thought, so I ran from them.

In 1984, I moved back home to New York City after I graduated from college. I quickly found an apartment and a job and began to forge a life of my own. Although my mother continued to drink heavily, I saw her when I could, hoping that someday something would cause her to stop abusing herself.

A few years later, something did, and my stormy relationship with my mother changed forever. Initially, it might have looked like another gigantic banana peel, but it ended up becoming a great gift. A true rainbow moment.

The mother I had grown up with, the mother whom I both loved and hated with a fierce passion, finally sobered up.

The memories of my childhood faded from my mind as I neared the house. At first, it seemed as if my walk hadn't helped. I can't write about this, I thought to myself. How is *this* positive?

Then, an idea hit me, and I raced into the house and up to my computer again.

As Robert H. Schuller once said, turn your scars into stars!

When I got to my office, I ran to my desk, grabbed the keyboard, and began to write.

CHAPTER FOUR

Turning Scars into Stars

I COULD FILL THIS BOOK with dysfunctional stories from my youth, but I won't. I have long forgiven my late parents, childhood bullies, and various dysfunctional friends and relatives.

The good news is that the ghosts from my childhood no longer haunt me.

The bad news is that I can dredge up in an instant the anger planted inside of me by those events. I was on Facebook a while back and found myself staring at a picture of a person I hadn't seen in years.

In the blink of an eye, I found myself back in the 1970s walking down an extremely unpleasant memory lane.

Although I had music on in my office, I was paying no attention to it because I was deep inside the memory. As the anger started to boil up inside me, the music suddenly broke through the haze of my anger and finally caught my attention.

Amazingly, it was the song "Let it Go."

Smiling, I pushed my chair back from my desk, shook my head from side to side, and looked up at the ceiling. Message received.

Let it go.

Exactly right.

Is it normal for a fifty-something-year-old woman to be sitting at her desk being angry at something that occurred more than thirty years ago?

I sat back down and wondered about it. Perhaps not, but yet I was doing exactly that. Let's ignore the fact that I really thought I had let it go years ago.

So here's how I turned my banana peel childhood into a rainbow:

I turned the scars into stars.

I finally realized that my past was *not* my destination and that I was the only person on the planet who could change that.

I banished my unhappy memories to the trash bin of my mind and conjured up the happy ones. I remembered our loving dogs and how much joy they brought me. I remembered happy moments with each of my parents and recalled some funny stories. I then wrote down every name that came to my mind and tried to see that person in a positive way. I tried to imagine these old friends, enemies, or family members as being happy and seeing smiles on all their faces. Then I forgave them all again. I realized that they had all done the best they could with the limited tools they had at the time.

In short, I remembered the love.

I also wrote a long letter to both my parents, various relatives, and those childhood bullies. I sent all my anger and emotion to those pages. Then I tore up the pages and tossed them into the garbage.

As the anger melted away in the happy memories, forgiveness finally came. It led me out of the banana peel field.

That's what it's all about, right?

Love.

At the end of the day, my parents loved me and did the best that they could. Were they perfect? Absolutely not. But neither am I. We are imperfect beings living in an imperfect world, yet we are all striving for perfection. We all want the rainbow of life that contains pure joy, happiness, and everything we ever wanted.

Being happy NOW. Being in joy NOW. That's the key to climbing back up onto that rainbow.

The reality of my youth was this: I had brilliant teachers who taught me, on an annoyingly consistent basis, what not to do. They were polishing me like tarnished silver. That small little thought allowed me to turn my scars into stars.

My advice? Try and learn from your past, just don't live there. Because the past is *not* your destination!

And when a picture or phone call causes me to slip off my rainbow again? I try and remind myself that they are teaching me, again, what not to do. I bless the experience for what it is and move on.

Now I dare you to do the same. Since there is nowhere you can go to escape from the ghosts of your past, I challenge you to face them and banish them forever.

I dare you to move beyond your past!

I dare you to change your life!

CHAPTER FIVE

From Drunk to Best Friend

I STOPPED TYPING AND LEANED back in my chair.

Scars.

Yes, I had them, I thought to myself. A bunch of them actually. You don't get to the age of fifty-three without some battle wounds.

A cold burst of air brushed over my face.

I'm going to have to turn up the heat in here, I thought to myself.

Just as I finished that thought, my mind went back to my mother.

She really was the best friend I ever had. As a tear ran down my cheek, the memory surfaced in my mind and before I could stop it, ancient ghosts threw me back to the year 1987.

It happened late one night. As usual, my mother had been drinking all day and was drunk. As she descended the stairs to the kitchen, she lost her balance and fell, breaking her hip in the process. Luckily, my older brother was there and got her safely to the hospital.

He called me. "I'm at the emergency room with Mom. You need to get here fast."

I grabbed a taxi and arrived at the hospital about twenty minutes later. As I walked into the emergency room, there she was. Drunk and in pain. I kissed her head, but she didn't even know I was there. A doctor greeted me, "Your mother is stable, but she will have to be admitted to the hospital for surgery. Once we detox her, we can operate. Does she drink like this often?"

What a question, I thought to myself.

"Unfortunately," I replied.

Certainly this incident was a tragedy, but it was ultimately the best thing that could have happened to my mother. It was the one thing that could actually force her to stop drinking. Even my mother couldn't find a way to sneak a gin and tonic into Lenox Hill Hospital with a broken hip.

So while she was in the hospital, I took this golden moment to arrange for a family "intervention." Since this was the second time in my life that I had tried to do this, I knew what to do and quickly put my plan into action. After I found her telephone book (there were no smart phones back then), I crossed my fingers and began to call her family and friends. One by one, I asked each of them if they could come to a family meeting at our house on the day she was released, and unlike the first time I tried this, they all agreed. I then called a rehabilitation center that I knew about, packed her bags, and arranged for a car service to take her there.

When Mom was finally released from the hospital a few weeks later, my brother and I brought her home and took her straight into the living room where her family and closest friends were waiting for her. We then confronted her about her drinking, and although she never completely accepted it, she still agreed to go to a rehab center. After the family meeting was over, we settled her into a car (before she had time to think about what she was doing) and whisked her to rehab.

It worked beautifully. My mother finally received the treatment she so desperately needed and became sober for the first time in her life.

My relationship with my mother had always been precarious at best when she was drinking, but when she stopped, she changed completely. And we quickly became fast friends.

She was so different sober.

The woman whom I had known for years was gone, replaced by a warm and caring individual who loved me with all her heart and soul.

Although I had always loved my mother, I never really liked her. Her drinking had made her into someone whom I just couldn't live with. Once sober, however, she became the mother who I had always wanted and had dreamed about for years. The person whom I had only seen brief glimpses of over the last twenty-five years had finally arrived.

And BAM . . .

I was back up on that beautiful, wonderful, slippery rainbow.

We talked about anything and everything, traveled together, and even bought a cooperative apartment in New York City together. We behaved more like sisters than mother and daughter. We went out to dinner, saw Broadway shows, went to art museums, and often talked far into the night about absolutely everything. It was almost as if we were trying to make up for a lifetime of mistakes and neglect as quickly as we could. We enjoyed each other's company so much that we never wanted it to end.

But it did end—and entirely too soon.

In the spring of 1990, my mother was diagnosed with cancer.

The news instantly pushed me off the rainbow, and I crashed into the banana peel field hard.

I stayed there for over a year.

Mom died from cancer on November 20, 1990, at the age of fifty-eight—three years after she achieved sobriety.

Just when I had finally found my mother—I lost her.

I shook my head to rid myself of the ghosts of the past and snapped back to the present, to the book I was writing. The memory was more than painful. It was bone crushing.

Anger, I thought to myself. I was angry for years after that.

Anger. Now *that*'s a good topic!

An idea popped into my mind, and I started typing again.

CHAPTER SIX

Your Glass of Anger

PICK UP A GLASS AND fill it with liquid. It can be any kind of liquid: water, iced tea, soda. Now hold it in front of you with your arm straight out and stay like that for a few minutes.

The glass you are holding represents your anger. The liquid inside the glass represents years and years of fear, resentment, and anger for the things people have done to you. For many of you, it's taken a long time to fill up your glass of anger, and for others the glass was just filled up yesterday.

When you first start getting angry, it's *really* easy to hold the glass up in front of me. I can balance my life with my anger because it's not affecting where I'm going. I can easily hold it off to the side. It's manageable. However, the longer that I hold this glass, the more my arm is going to tire and eventually hurt.

Soon, my arm is going to really start to ache, and it's going to get harder and harder to hold up the glass. When I first lifted it, I could easily hold it off to the side, but now that my arm is hurting, I can't. In fact, I can't focus on anything but the glass anymore. It's affecting every part of my life now, as the pain is more than I can bear. I'm talking about it to everyone, crying, whining, yelling, screaming, and shouting to everyone who can hear me. I'm also getting resentful about the fact that I have to hold up this damn glass.

The glass of anger has wormed its way into every part of my life now. The longer I hold onto it, the more painful it's going to get. In fact, after a while, I'm going to have to use my other arm to help me hold up the glass.

Now, look at your body language. My life hasn't stopped *exactly* because I can still *sort of* see beyond the glass in front of me. That's about it, though, because both my arms are now dedicated to holding up the glass.

If I continue to hold up the glass of anger, and I don't forgive, and I don't let go, and I don't put it down, eventually it's going to affect where I'm going because it's going to be right in front of me. The pain is now so intense that the anger is all I can see. I can't hold it off to the side any longer. And if you're still stubborn and are dead set against letting go of the anger and you think that you can manage it all, after a while your little glass of anger is going to turn into a pitcher of anger.

It's going to grow!

The pitcher is worse, of course, because the pitcher of anger that I am holding onto is so big it is now all I can see. I'm now missing opportunities that are being presented to me.

My soul mate might have just walked into the room, but because I'm holding on to the pitcher of anger, I can't see this ideal person and he or she walks away. My dream job, a potential new and fabulous house, a cure for my illness, or a great life-changing opportunity could all appear in front of me and I won't see them because I'm still focused on the anger, which is now a *huge* pitcher.

Ideas, things, people, places, none of it's going to happen because all I can focus on is that pitcher of anger I am stubbornly holding on to. My entire life is now focused on the fear, anger, hatred, and resentments that are inside that pitcher.

So what's inside of your glass of anger?

Is the anger stemming from your childhood? From someone in particular? From something someone did or didn't do? Because you are sick, lonely, hungry?

Whatever it is, it is holding you back.

So, how do you get rid of the anger inside the glass?

You already know the answer: forgiveness and gratitude.

It's time. Seriously.

Now, please allow me to be completely clear: Forgiving someone does *not* mean that they were right, nor does it mean that you want a relationship with them. Forgiving someone means that there is less anger in your glass and you can finally put the glass down. You might not want to talk to this person, but you've forgiven him or her and you're not resentful and angry anymore. You can finally look at their name on a piece of paper and you don't feel the anger rise up into the back of your throat and choke you.

Now look at your body language. With the glass or pitcher down, you can finally see things around you. Your hands are now free so you can do things. You'll see the opportunities that are flowing to you. Ideas will now flood your brain, and new roads will appear in your path. Why? Because the ideas were *trying* to flow into your mind, but they were being stopped at the gate because of the anger. You unconsciously pushed the new ideas into the back of your mind because all you could focus on was the anger and resentment inside the glass. You lived it, breathed it, drank it in.

So put down your glass of anger.

It's time, don't you think?

You have suffered enough.

Forgive the people inside the glass.

Who should you start with? The person you are thinking about right now as you read these words.

"You know, Katharine, I HAVE forgiven them!" You might now be saying to me.

Possibly.

Consider this: If you really *have* completely forgiven them, then why are they entering your mind now as you read these words? Sometimes you have to forgive people more than once. In fact, you might have to do it a bunch of times, especially if the person is family or you live with this person.

"Well, I can't put down my glass of anger and forgive because I'm blocked!"

I hate the word "blocked."

Would you like to know why?

Mostly because the word itself is a block. Just the mere fact that you are telling me you are blocked is a block.

"I am blocked"—possibly the strongest affirmation in the world—is guaranteed to make you stay right where you are. It stops all forward motion because you start to obsess about it. It's all you can think and talk about. You live it and breathe it in every day, searching for that one piece of magical information that will get rid of it.

So you stay blocked because you *think* you are blocked.

I just hate that word.

Plus, even if you do figure out what it is that has made you angry, you still have that small voice in the back of your mind that wonders if you really did find out what it was because a few months from now you'll find yourself in another dark place and the "block" roller coaster will start all over again.

So here's what I do: I replace the word "block" with "distractions."

What is distracting you from attaining your dreams?

Let's start by writing down what is distracting you right now.

You have work to do for your boss?

Your can't get dysfunctional childhood memories out of your head?

Your friends told you that you can't?

You're in a bad relationship?

You have no money in the bank?

You are sick?

Distractions. I can't put down my glass of anger because I have too many distractions right now and I can't focus on it.

Let's take a look at that last one: You are sick. You are too sick to start moving toward your dream.

Okay, I respect that. Stage 3 breast cancer was a *huge* distraction for me. Being sick for two years was horrible. However, I never let my illness prevent me from writing my blog, talking with friends, or consulting with clients— all of which brings me incredible joy. Life is just too darn short to not live in your joy.

So what is distracting you?

Lack of money?

There's a good one!

"I don't have enough money to start."

Okay, fine, your bank account has a $1.50 in it. I get that.

I also understand that the Internet is free, and you can do some research on your dream (or your current distraction) without spending a dime. There is information out there on every topic you can possibly imagine.

What is your *heart* telling you to do? Your gut? Your inner voice?

What was your knee-jerk reaction when I asked what is distracting you? What was the first thing that popped into your mind?

Start there.

Choose to move forward through your distractions.

Choose to feel the sun on your face, have more than enough money in your bank account, a healthy body, and a happy relationship. Choose this in your mind and then feel the results. Smile about it. Daydream about it. Where would you go if your dream was given to you *right now*? Daydream about that.

Do that every day.

Think *positive,* forward-moving thoughts that include loving words such as certain, capable, and happy.

Eventually, people will magically float into your life that will help you get where you want to go, and the negative ones who are holding you back will float out. You will stumble across websites and articles that will inspire you with ideas. You'll see something on television or hear it in a song on the radio. Distractions that took over your life yesterday will disappear today, and you'll be walking in a new direction.

Then you'll be on your way.

So stop saying that you are blocked!

You are not blocked; you are just temporarily distracted.

Your life might look gloomy and miserable now, but remember that the sun always comes out after a rainstorm, so hang in there.

Do what I do—when I get into that dark place and random negative situations hit me, I look at the situation as my launching pad to something even greater.

Sure, I was sick for two years, but if I hadn't gone through it, I wouldn't be here with you right now.

After your little glass of anger is empty, bless the energy and then stand your ground. Don't go back and fill up your glass again. Stand your ground! If you can do that, eventually you can use the experience as a launching pad to something even greater. The hurt is a teacher that shows you things about yourself that help you to grow. That's the silver lining. You grow and become greater.

CHAPTER SEVEN

The Anger Merry-go-round

I ABRUPTLY STOPPED TYPING.

Putting down my little glass of anger is all well and good, I thought, but what do you do when you get to those last few drops in the glass? That *one* person who you have forgiven over and over and over?

Since no answers were flying into my mind, I decided to stop writing and try again tomorrow. I saved the document and walked downstairs.

A hundred things needed my attention when I got there. Two sons home from college bring a myriad of chores for a mom to do. Since buying groceries was at the top of my list, and the fact that I really needed to clear my head, I grabbed my keys and drove to the grocery store.

As I walked around the grocery store, my mind wandered to the question of the day. How do you forgive and move on when you are related to the person who angers you so? How many times can you forgive that person? The answer to that had eluded me for years.

Actually, I have forgiven some people more times than I can count. The trouble for me is that whenever I see or hear their name, the past comes boiling back up into the back of my throat and the memories choke me once again.

I can't write this chapter until I figure this out, I thought as I pushed my shopping cart around the store.

When I got home, my husband was in his office working. I put the groceries away and walked in and sat down in the chair next to his desk.

"I can't do it. I can't write about forgiveness," I blurted out randomly.

"Why not?" he calmly asked.

"I'm blocked," I grinned broadly.

He just stared at me. He knew exactly who I was talking about, and I could see him bracing for another long conversation. We'd been married for more than twenty-two years, so this issue was not exactly new to him.

"Why don't you just stop?"

"What do you mean stop?" I asked.

"Just walk away. Stop. Give yourself a break," he said. "Listen, there are two things that are never going to change here. First, this is always going to piss you off. Second, the reality of this situation is that you *have* forgiven them. You just haven't moved on from it. So just stop. Your problem is not forgiving; your problem is that you can't move on. You're stuck in a loop."

My jaw just about dropped to the floor. He was right. I had just spent twenty-plus years on the anger merry-go-round and the only person it was hurting was *me*! The reality was that I was the only one losing sleep.

"Kath, it's a process. Listen, someone will always be able to push your buttons and make you angry. It's what you do with that anger that matters. So toss it as it comes to you, forgive yourself, forgive them, and then move on!"

I kissed my husband and went back to my office.

A few minutes later, a good friend texted me, asking how I was. Since forgiveness was on my mind at that moment, I told her what I was thinking. Her reply was so similar to Ron's that I almost fell out of my chair.

"I've been in that movie!" she texted. "Now I control my reactions. Often they don't know how angry I am and who is that really hurting? Me!"

What an "ah-ha" moment.

It was only then that I finally realized that forgiveness comes in stages. I have forgiven those people in my life (over and over actually but who's counting?), but now it's time to walk away from it.

It's time to concentrate on my family.

For me, family is an extremely sacred word that I reserve for the very special people in my life. My family is large and contains people whom I choose to be with. They have my back, and I have theirs. Some share my blood; some don't. My family is closer than close, closer than blood if that's at all possible.

My family shares my soul.

The anger merry-go-round. What a waste of time, I thought. It's time to get off this ride and back up on the rainbow.

I started typing again.

CHAPTER EIGHT

Wallow, Rinse, and Repeat

WHY DID IT TAKE ME so long to forgive?

It wasn't because I couldn't.

Quite frankly, it was because I simply didn't want to. I wanted to stay angry.

I was too committed to "my story" to give it up. It had become my identity. My new normal, so to speak. Besides, if I didn't have "my story," then who exactly would I be? It was too scary a thought to even consider.

My story featured a heroine who was a survivor of a toxic alcoholic family. My story had a bunch of different chapters in it. From family problems and divorce to money trouble and health issues, it was all there.

I was a survivor, and I had happily wallowed in it for years. As time went on, long-held resentments frequently drifted into the front of my mind, and I often got lost in the memories. I was negative all the time, angry at the world in general, and completely miserable.

I honestly had no idea how to get out of the hell that I was in.

I could have changed my life, but it was easier to stay the way I was: angry, unhealthy, and emotionally poor. It was familiar. I was used to it.

It wasn't until I hit my late thirties, that I finally began to understand that my anger was holding me back and the resentments were making me sick. Literally. I had stomach issues, got colds and the flu easily, and often felt poorly. Money was an issue all the time, and my stress level was high.

Something had to give.

I changed when I finally realized that I needed to lose the story and forgive them for *me*. I wanted to stop thinking about them all the time. I didn't want a relationship with them; I just wanted to be free. They had taken up space in my head and were living there rent free.

Time to evict!

What I finally came to understand was that forgiveness comes in stages. Forgiveness is a journey. It's a long staircase that has several levels in it. The trick is to keep going and not stay too long on each landing.

Below are the three levels of forgiveness that I have come up with. It took me a long time to realize that you just can't forgive some people right away. It's a process that takes time to achieve. I did achieve it and eventually was able to get to stage three and move on, but it didn't happen overnight.

You can do this. Be kind to yourself. Know that anger is normal. You'll move on when you are ready.

KATHARINE'S THREE LEVELS OF FORGIVENESS

1. "I forgive you." It's just words. You don't really mean it. I forgive you, but I'm not forgetting. Your glass of anger is totally full right now; in fact, it's overflowing, and it's going to stay that way for a long while. What you're really saying is, *I know I should forgive you, but I can't completely because, honestly, I'm still angry.*

2. Now, you have some feeling attached to the words. Your glass of anger is only half-full so you're making progress. You're going to try and forgive because you need to be free. At this stage "I forgive you" means: *Your name still brings up anger, but not as badly as it used to. I can manage it. I really think I*

have forgiven you, but I can't seem to move on from it. I'm working on it.

3. The words are gone and have been replaced by feeling. Your glass of anger is empty now. Finally, you can say, *Although I might not want a relationship with you, I completely and totally forgive you. I can let go and move on now. I am free.*

So what do you do right now?

I suggest that you get a mental picture in your mind of the person with whom you are angry.

What are you feeling?

Are you still incredibly angry?

Can you forgive that person?

Do you *want* to forgive him or her? It's fine if you don't.

What is your heart telling you?

Remember, forgiving someone does *not* mean he or she was right. It simply means that you are sick and tired of being angry and wish to move on. You want to put down your glass of anger.

There are tons of books and websites on forgiveness and anger that will help you move through this process if you wish more information.

You can do this.

CHAPTER NINE

One Door Closes, Another Opens

I LEANED BACK IN MY chair and stopped typing again.

As I gazed out my office window, I took a sip of tea and watched a mother with a stroller walk by the house.

My mother. I thought to myself. A gracious and wonderful woman who died entirely too soon.

Much too soon, I thought sadly.

Forgiveness played loudly in the last three years of her life as we both forgave each other for decades of madness.

As the thought entered my brain, my mind started to go back in time. This time to the year 1990.

Now *that* year was a pile of crap, I thought to myself. A gigantic banana peel field that took me a long time to get out of.

The memory held onto me fast and I was soon lost in it.

I was in my late twenties and working for a nonprofit association in New York City when my mother contracted cancer. It was caught too late. By the time the doctors found it, it was deep into Stage 4 and had spread everywhere.

After a few weeks or so in the hospital, Mom came home to live with me in my small one-bedroom apartment. Since my brother had just gotten married and I was still single, we all agreed that I was the logical choice to care for her. Although we all suggested hospice, she refused to have anything to do with it. So she moved in with me. My brother and I then arranged for a hospital bed and two nurses to stay with her around the clock. I went to work during the day and spent evenings with my mother. I took her to her chemotherapy treatments when I could, spent hours reading to her, bathed her, did all the laundry, cooked the meals, and generally helped her through the pain of it all.

I saw no friends and didn't date. The only person I talked to was my brother. My entire focus in those days was to simply be with my mother in her time of need. The person I cared about the most, the person who had been my best friend in the world needed me desperately. This wonderful woman had devoted her life to me despite her own personal demons and had helped me through my own personal trials and illnesses. Even during her alcoholic years, my mother was always there when I needed her, so now it was my turn to be there for her. After all, it was certainly the least I could do for the person who gave me life, unconditional love, and true friendship.

During those horrible weeks, we talked about everything. We tried to cram an entire lifetime of words into a few brief moments of time. She talked about her years as an alcoholic and apologized to me over and over again. She spoke about our family history, and we wrote down the family tree so that it wouldn't be forgotten. She gave me recipes and lessons in cooking, advice on marriage and childrearing, and simply tried to share as much as she could during the few moments we had left with each other. She even helped me sort out my feelings about my father.

Mom went through all the phases of illness: disbelief, fear, anger, acceptance. Even though I was the brunt of her anger more often than not, I accepted what she dished out to me, for I knew that she didn't really mean some of the things she said and was simply lashing out at any human who happened to be nearby. Usually me. Although I have to admit, it was sometimes extremely hard to bear.

Three months later, my entire world came apart at the seams on the night that she died.

I remember racing home from the office that day with the sinking feeling that I needed to get home fast. When I arrived, I took one look and knew that her time had finally come. I called my brother and his wife, and they came immediately. Incredibly, it was as if Mom was purposely waiting for the three of us to get home before she died.

As my sister-in-law and I held her hands, my brother stroked her forehead. Since I was incapable of speech, he whispered soft, loving words of endearment to her. The tears rolled down my cheeks unchecked as he whispered into her ears.

"Mom, it's okay," he said lovingly. "We're fine. You can go now. You can be at peace. It's okay to leave now. We love you."

Then we all simply watched her body shut down and the breath leave her for the last time. It wasn't like the deaths that you see in the movies. There were no prophetic last words and no momentous happenings. It was peaceful and dignified. She just quietly sank into the deep sleep of death, and the marks of pain that she had endured for months finally faded from her face.

She was fifty-eight.

My brother and sister-in-law both tell me that they actually saw her soul leave her body when she died and have said that it was like a white light rushing out of her body toward the heavens.

I didn't see anything of the sort. All I saw was the blood dripping out of the side of her mouth. As I watched it trickle slowly down her face, my whole world fell apart. That single drop of blood tore my very soul into thousands of tiny pieces. It didn't seem real to me until that exact moment. The pure anguish that I felt ripped me apart both inside and out. The little girl in me was shouting, "No, Mommy, you can't die yet!" and I wanted to shake her to wake her up again.

How could she leave me now? I just found her!

I remember sinking to my knees, screaming at the top of my lungs and sobbing as my brother caught me and held me in his arms. My mind went in a hundred different directions and seemed to explode when the last breath left her body. I was hysterical and couldn't focus on anything.

When our minister and the coroner arrived, they tried their best to steer me into the bedroom to avoid seeing her being taken out of the apartment in a body bag, but I saw it anyway. It was when I heard the sound of the zipper that I knew it was final.

My best friend was gone forever, and I was completely alone in the world.

I spent the next eight months adrift. I had no purpose and walked around in the deep, black fog of mourning. I went to work, of course, but I didn't see friends. I didn't date. I went through life on auto-pilot.

I didn't care what happened to me.

I was deep inside the banana peel field, and I didn't care. I didn't want to leave it. I didn't want to get out. I saw no future for myself and was content to stay where I was in the middle of the field.

After a few months of this, my sister-in-law called. "I think you should rent a share in a house in the Hamptons."

"What is that?" I replied robotically. I was really just humoring her as I had no intention of leaving my apartment.

"You rent a share in a house, and you can go every other weekend during the summer. It will be good for you to get out of the city. You've been alone in that apartment long enough. You need to get out, Kath."

"Why? I'm perfectly fine. Plus, I won't know anybody in the Hamptons. Seriously, I really don't want to."

"Why not? You'll have fun. Remember fun? Remember smiling?" she replied firmly.

I think she and my brother were hoping that the Hamptons might kick some life back into me. It was a chance to go to the beach, meet people, and make some new friends. At the very least, it got me out of the hot city every other weekend.

I wish they would leave me alone, I thought grumpily as I put down the telephone. Deep inside I knew she was right, though. I sat there for what seemed like hours, and then with a sigh, I picked up the phone and made the call.

The following weekend, I hopped onto the Hampton Jitney for my first weekend. What I remember most about that first weekend is the fear. When I got off the Jitney in Quogue, I have never been so scared in my life. Being a naturally shy person, fear gripped me the minute

I stepped off the bus. I found myself all alone at a bus stop, staring at the road ahead of me long after the bus pulled away. I was walking into a house where I didn't know a soul, and I was scared out of my mind. Since my hands were shaking so badly, I stuffed one of them into my pants pocket, picked up my bag, and began to walk.

As I walked down the road toward the house, my heart started racing, and I started to have trouble breathing. The closer the house got, the more panicked I became. Yet incredibly, I kept moving forward toward the house. Something deep down inside of me whispered to me to keep going, and I listened to it.

Damn, I thought. I *really* don't want to do this. Fear continued to hold me as I continued down the road.

Eventually, I got to the house and walked up the stairs. It was a huge Victorian house with a wide front porch. Since the door was unlocked, and there was no doorbell that I could see, I took a deep breath and walked right in. As I entered the foyer, I heard people talking in the kitchen. With my heart pounding in my chest, I put my small bag down in the hall, wandered into the big kitchen, and quietly said hello to the first person I saw. Thankfully, she couldn't have been nicer, and before I knew it, I was sitting at the table with a cup of coffee in my hand. She then guided me upstairs and showed me to my room. As I put my bag down on the bed, I met my roommate Barbara, and we chatted for a few minutes. The fear that had gripped me only an hour before started to melt away, and I found I was finally able to breathe again.

Perhaps this won't be too bad, I thought to myself.

Over the course of the next few weekends, I made some friends and had a nice time every time I went up there.

Incredibly, about a month later I finally got out of the banana peel field and amazingly found myself back up on the rainbow.

I'll never forget that day.

I remember a man walking toward me on the beach. It was a beautiful sunny day, and I was there with a huge group of people who all had shares in the house I was staying in.

The man approaching us was big with strong-looking arms and a nicely toned body. He walked with a slight limp. He smiled at everyone and said a cheerful hello. My friends all greeted him warmly, and several moved over so that he could sit down. Within seconds, he had everyone in the group laughing loudly.

What a handsome man, I thought to myself. You could just feel the strength coming off him, and I found myself staring. Since my towel was the farthest from where he was sitting, combined with the fact that I was painfully shy, we never spoke to each other. Yet I couldn't take my eyes off of him. He was different somehow. I could feel it.

As I quietly watched him, I wondered if he was dating anyone. I dismissed the thought quickly, as I was pretty sure someone would have snatched him up by now.

The following morning, I rose from my bed, grabbed my glasses, ran a comb through my hair, and wandered downstairs in search of coffee. It never occurred to me to put on makeup or shower as I wasn't there to find a boyfriend. I just wanted to be left alone to wallow in my grief.

The man from the beach was there. When I walked into the kitchen, he was standing by the coffee pot right next to Barbara. Like the day before, everyone around him was laughing.

I wanted to run back to my room and hide, but something inside of me gently nudged my back and I kept walking. As I gingerly reached for a coffee cup, my friend introduced us.

"Kath, this is Ron. Ron this is my new friend Kath," Barbara said.

"Hello," I replied nervously.

"Hi," he said smiling warmly.

"We're having a beach barbeque tonight and need some corn shucked. Would you two like to help?" As Barbara said it, she gave me the most penetrating stare I had ever seen. As if to say, don't argue with me.

"Certainly. No problem," Ron quickly replied, and we both went over to the garbage can to begin work.

As we shucked corn, we chatted about all sorts of topics. His easy personality quickly drew me in, and before I knew it, I felt like I had known him all my life. It certainly didn't hurt that he was easy on the eyes either.

At the beach that night, he quickly found me when he arrived at the party, and we spent the entire evening together talking late into the night.

The next day Ron drove Barbara and me home to the city. As he dropped me off at my apartment, he politely asked for my phone number, and I happily gave it to him.

As I walked into the building, I wondered if I would ever see him again.

I did. He called a few days later, and we went out to dinner. It was a lovely evening with great Italian food. Afterwards, we took a walk and strolled down the New York City streets. It was a simple evening and just what I needed. He was fun to be with, and we talked like we had been friends for years.

Two weeks later, I was back in the Hamptons. True to his word, Ron had called me several times during the past few weeks, and I happily agreed to meet and go on our second date.

He picked me up bright and early that Saturday morning, and we spent the entire day with each other. We drove all over the Hamptons, occasionally stopping for food or coffee. Twelve hours later, we ended up on the tip of Long Island in Montauk eating clams at a little roadside restaurant. Ron was warm, friendly, and extremely funny. He patiently listened to me while I spoke of my mother and offered insightful advice when I finished.

It was like the light finally came back on, and I didn't want the day to end. I didn't want to go back to the darkness of my life.

As it turns out, I didn't have to because exactly one year later I married him.

So what force kept me moving forward that day so long ago? How did I get through it?

I trusted my gut. My intuition. My inner compass, if you will. I intuitively knew I had to do it, and I knew it would somehow change my life.

Besides, what was the alternative? Live alone in my apartment with only the television for company for the rest of my life? I didn't want to die with my mother; I wanted to live!

I was also willing to change, even though the mere thought of change scared the wits out of me. Deep down inside I knew I couldn't go back, even if I wanted to.

I smiled as the memory faded from my mind.

What a brilliant rainbow that was, I thought to myself. That memory was a beautiful gift.

Ron was certainly one of my lighthouses.

Lighthouses!

I took a sip of tea and started typing again.

CHAPTER TEN

Treasure the Lighthouses: For Without Their Light, Our Ships Would Crash on the Rocks

JUST LIKE THERE ARE MOMENTS of time that change your life, there are also people. Everyone knows that the lighthouse is there to guide ships safely into the harbor. What many don't know is that this idea can be applied to people as well.

Everyone has a lighthouse in his or her life. These lighthouses are people who steer us through the storms of life and provide a light for us to follow out of the darkness. They show us how to negotiate the "rocks" and navigate through the fog and severe storms that come along in our lives. Without them, we would almost certainly crash on the rocks.

I know I would have.

I have had several lighthouses in my life including my husband, Ron. Without these incredible people, I wouldn't be here with you today and would have wrecked on the rocks long ago. I could go on and on about these people and what they have done for me, but it's the story of one lighthouse, in particular, that I would like to share with you now.

It was a rainy and cold night in New York City sometime in the late 1960s. The wind was roaring around the street corners, and the rain was pouring down onto the sidewalk in sheets. On this particular night, my elderly great-grandmother was trying to get home from the grocery store. She was attempting to walk down Park Avenue and had her cane in one hand and her little bag of groceries in the other. Walking was hard for her on a good day, so a day like this one made it almost impossible. When she was about halfway home, a long, black stretch limousine pulled up to the curb and stopped next to her. The door opened, and a woman got out of the car. Ignoring the rain that soon soaked her through, the woman walked right up to my great-grandmother and gently asked if she could give her a ride home. Shortly after, my great-grandmother was settled comfortably in the back of the limousine and was driven home.

The woman?

Carol Burnett.

As a child, I used to listen to my parents tell this story, and I can distinctly remember deciding to become just like Carol Burnett when I grew up. The money and fame aspect of her life meant nothing to me; it was her other traits that I aspired to. The love and genuine compassion that she showed to my great-grandmother that night was the person who I wanted to be. I wanted to be funny and loving. I wanted to help people and be warm and honest.

Quite frankly, she was my lighthouse, and her bright light guided me through my stormy teenage years. As I navigated through the many rocks and storms that came up, I kept my eye on my lighthouse. Carol Burnett became my north star, and she guided me safely into my twenties, where I picked up another lighthouse to guide me on my journey.

Many years later, when I was about eight months pregnant with my first son, I finally found the chance to pass it forward. I was headed to the grocery store when I saw an old lady pushing a cart filled with groceries. She had twisted and thin little legs and seemed to struggle with each step. So I pulled my car over to the side of the road and got out with the intention of helping the woman home. As I walked up to her, I offered my help and guess what happened?

She hit me on the head with her umbrella and screamed, "I can do it myself!"

As I got into my car, I laughed until tears came to my eyes. Oh well, I thought, I suppose you can't help everyone. Carol Burnett would love this story, I thought.

Now that I'm all grown up, I have indeed passed it forward many times since those days long ago, and I hope to continue to do so in the future.

My lighthouse gave an extremely angry teenager a positive direction in which to walk when I could have so easily taken the wrong path. She showed me where to step during the storms that followed over the years and made me laugh when I needed some extra light. I watched as she went through her own trials and tribulations with dignity, love, grace, and incredible courage. I have tried to do the same when my own trials came across my path. I could have walked in all sorts of directions in those early formative years, but her light showed me the way. As time went on, several more lighthouses appeared to guide me through and I have finally made it safely to the harbor.

Now, let's talk about each one of you. Who were the lighthouses of your life? How did they help you get across the ocean? Each one of us has had a lighthouse to guide us through life, and I think it's important to look back and recognize them so that we can give them our thanks and our love.

Today, I like to think that I'm a lighthouse. I think everyone should be a lighthouse for someone because the light that you share could change that person's life forever.

So stand tall and proud and shine your light far and wide. Plant your feet firmly into the ground like an oak tree and guide people where they need to go. And if they choose to sail out of the harbor? Let them. They'll be back one day.

CHAPTER ELEVEN

The Cancer Fields

I PAUSED, LEANED BACK IN my chair, and reread what I'd just written. Since it was getting dark outside, I went downstairs, cracked open an ice-cold O'Doul's, and looked for Ron. I was tired and needed to think about something else for a while. He suggested we go out for a quick dinner. Perfect, I said.

The following morning I was at my desk again.

Change. That's what the last two decades were all about, I thought, and it wasn't always pretty. I wasn't kidding when I said I've slipped on some serious banana peels in my life.

As I gazed out my office window, my mind started to wander back to the biggest banana peel field of my life. Within minutes, the memories took me back to the week before my fiftieth birthday.

I woke up as I usually do and headed straight for the coffee pot. A few minutes later, I was sitting at our kitchen table reading the newspaper when I got the strangest urge.

I felt like I should take up jogging.

Not earth shattering for most of you, but considering I have been severely allergic to exercise my *entire* life, this was a serious thought for me.

Ron couldn't believe it.

For days, I tried to banish the thought from mind, but I couldn't. I just couldn't shake the feeling in my gut that I *had* to start jogging.

God, it seemed, for whatever reason *really* wanted me to get some exercise.

So thinking I was having a mid-life crisis, a few days later I updated my status on Facebook and casually mentioned that I was thinking about taking up jogging. A friend immediately commented that I should try the Couch-to-5K® Running Plan.

Why not? I thought.

So off I went. For the next year, I ran every other day and managed to get myself up to two miles. Fantastic! I just loved it. On my runs, I listened to great music and meditated. It was a chance to be with nature and contemplate my life.

About halfway through the year, the weight started to come off of me. I went from a size 12–14 to a 10, and by March 2012, I was down to an 8. I thought it was great!

There was a darkness to the weight loss, though, and I instinctively knew it. Something wasn't right. The weight was coming off too fast. My cheeks were sinking into my face, and my clothes were hanging on me. Even my engagement ring didn't fit anymore.

On May 19, 2012, the day before my birthday, I found myself entering the darkest banana peel field of my life. I was in the shower when I found the lump on my left side. More than a little startled, I dried myself off, put on a robe, and found Ron. Although it was in a very strange place, he felt it, too.

On the morning of May 21, I was in the doctor's office.

"That's definitely a lump," she said after examining me. "Why don't you sit here, and I'll make a few calls." She put her hand on my shoulder and gave me a warm smile. She then twirled around and bolted for the door.

Bolted!

Okay, the fact that my doctor just ran out of the examination room is probably *not* a good sign, I thought miserably.

For the next few hours, I was scanned, poked, and prodded by a battery of people. Apparently, I fell in the 10 percent of people who had such dense breasts that mammograms didn't work on me.

Wish I had known that *before*.

They could all feel the lump; they just couldn't see it. Eventually, they did a sonogram and found it.

I knew it was bad when the radiologist himself asked me if I needed a referral for a good surgeon.

"No, thank you. My doctor has already set me up with one," I politely replied.

"Good. You should see them this week," he said. "Tomorrow would be good."

His body language told me that it was bad.

Damn.

As I left his office, he turned to me and shook my hand.

"Your doctor should have the results in a few days. Good luck, Mrs. Giovanni."

It felt like a death sentence.

As I walked to my car, I wondered how long I had to live. I didn't mention this exchange to Ron, but it haunted me for days.

By the next morning, we were at the surgeon's office getting a biopsy. Afterwards, she spent several minutes telling us what would happen if it was cancer.

Both Ron and the doctor were trying to be positive, but in my heart, I already knew it was cancer. The lump was just too large to be anything else. Besides, I was not feeling particularly well and was tired all the time.

We spoke for a few minutes more, then Ron and I left.

"You know, this lump is in such an odd spot, that if I hadn't taken up jogging and lost all that weight, I would never have found it," I randomly blurted out to Ron in the car.

"It's a good thing you do self-exams," he said. His eyes stayed on the road, but I could hear the emotion in his voice. He was desperately trying to remain calm.

"Running literally saved my life. If I hadn't listened to God's voice in my head, I might be dead."

"Yes, but you're not. Plus, we don't have the test results yet, so don't worry until we have something to worry about," he replied.

"Yes, but what if it *is* cancer? Did I catch it in time?"

"Let's not worry until we know the results." Unable to speak any further, we drove the rest of the way home in stunned silence.

As luck would have it, I was really busy for the next few days. It was a blessing as it took my mind off of my prognosis for a while. My oldest son was graduating from high school, and I had to fly to Portland a few days later to do a customer-service workshop. I knew that with my luck, the doctor would call with the lab results while I was in Portland, and I didn't need the distraction while I was speaking to a group. The timing was horrible, but the show must go on.

As I packed my suitcase, I stuffed the cancer and everything that word implied to the back of my mind.

"Please don't call me when I'm in Portland," I told Ron as we drove to the airport.

"Why not?" he replied.

"Because I know you too well. If the doctor calls and the test results are positive, I'll hear it in your voice and I won't be able to do this workshop. So just text me instead. Okay?"

"I understand. No problem," he said.

For the rest of the trip we talked about everything and nothing, just enjoying being with each other. The possibility of cancer had already changed our lives, and we understood how fragile life could be.

As I leaned in to give him a kiss good-bye, I could see the pain in his eyes, and it crushed me. Deep down, he knew it was bad, too. I could see it written all over his face.

We hugged each other tighter than ever when he dropped me off. Since I didn't want him to see me crying, I turned away quickly and strode into the terminal. A tear ran down my cheek unchecked as I searched for my gate.

When I arrived in Portland, Ron kept his word and texted me the entire time. He purposely kept his texts loving, positive, and motivational. Although the hotel was extremely nice, I barely noticed as I paced my room back and forth. My mind was racing, and I couldn't stem the dark thoughts that kept creeping into my mind. I texted Ron for over an hour and then spent another hour on the phone with my close friend, Lisa Ann. They were my lifeline to sanity and kept me grounded and sane so that I could conduct the workshop the following morning.

The gig in Portland went really well, and I flew home happy that the client was pleased with the workshop.

When I landed, I went to baggage claim and waited for my bag. I knew Ron was outside in the car waiting for me because I texted him from the plane when we landed. I also intuitively knew what he was going to say when I saw him.

I grabbed my bag off the carousel and took a deep breath to center myself. To stop my hand from shaking, I stuffed it in my pocket and walked as calmly as I could to the revolving door. I saw Ron standing by the car the minute I got outside.

His face told me the whole story.

No words were spoken. We just hugged each other and cried.

Stage 3 breast cancer. Triple positive.

The disease that killed my grandmother and my mother.

As we silently drove home, I asked myself the million dollar question: How much time do I have left?

I shook my head to rid myself of the memory and stared blankly at the computer in front of me.

Cancer. What a life-changing word.

As a tear began to quietly fall down my cheek, I began to type again.

CHAPTER TWELVE

The Four Words that Changed My Life

IT'S AMAZING HOW QUICKLY YOUR perspective can change. In my case, it changed in a matter of minutes. It only took four little words to completely shatter my world and change my life forever.

You have breast cancer.

Cancer.

The big "C."

No one thinks that it will happen to them. In fact, dying is something far in the future that we all know is going to happen, but certainly not today.

Cancer is something that happens to other people, right?

Breast cancer. Certainly a death sentence twenty years ago but thankfully not one today.

While I am positive that I'll be around for many years to come, my perspective has changed. The little things that used to bother me don't matter so much anymore, and I tell my family and friends how much they mean to me on a daily basis. I relish the days I can be home with my family, and I am grateful for the times I can be in my office doing what I love.

We all take health for granted. Actually, we take a *lot* of things for granted. Most of us will get up every morning and think about all the things that we have to do and then we'll get stressed out and sick as we rush through the day like a runaway freight train.

Me? I'm grateful for every morning that I wake up. The day is a gift to me now. I look forward to each day and try to help as many people as I can, whether I'm in the grocery store, on the telephone, writing e-mail, or posting on the Internet. It doesn't matter anymore, I'll help as many as I can. I'll offer a smile, a helping hand, or some encouraging words.

Don't take the day for granted. Spend today living life to its fullest. Be happy and grateful for everything that you have now. One moment of gratitude can change the course of your day in a second.

If you're in a banana peel field, then stay positive and keep your eye on the edge of the field—the future that you want. How do you want it to play out? Write the script. Write down exactly how you want it to happen. Then keep reading your script every day.

And me?

I practice what I preach and have already written my script. I'm also staying positive because fear and hate won't help me. It's not always easy, though, as my mind can go to the dark side of cancer in a heartbeat. Sometimes being positive is a minute-by-minute effort. It's like recovery—you have to take it one day at a time.

So stay positive, everyone, and please don't take waking up tomorrow for granted. It's a gift. A brand new day to change your life.

CHAPTER THIRTEEN

I Don't Want to Die

"IT'S CANCER. STAGE 3 TRIPLE positive," the surgeon said.

As Dr. Ndidi Azikiwe spoke to me about my options, I saw her lips moving but strangely I couldn't hear anything. I nodded my head as if I heard her, but I didn't. My mind was racing, and fear was taking over my entire body.

As a child, I was taught to keep a stiff upper lip in public and to show strength. The lessons served me well here, as I took the news as stoically as I could. I nodded politely and listened to her as calmly as possible.

I wasn't really paying attention, though, because inside my mind, I was screaming like a maniac!

WHY ME? I don't want to die!

"Now, we can treat this conservatively; you have options," the doctor continued.

The words grabbed my attention, and I immediately snapped back into the conversation. Abruptly, I interrupted her right in the middle of her sentence.

"With all due respect. No. We are not going to do anything conservatively. I want you to do a double mastectomy as soon as you can book an operating table. Monday morning would be perfect," I said. "Breast cancer runs in my family. Both my grandmothers and my mother died from breast cancer. I intend to survive this!"

"That's a great attitude," she said. "I can certainly fast-track you."

"How much time do I have left?" I couldn't help but ask.

"A lot," she reassured me. "With proper treatment, you can live for many years."

She continued talking about treatment and spoke about chemotherapy, radiation, reconstruction, and the many surgeries I would have, but I wasn't listening. I couldn't listen. I was numb. In shock. I saw her speaking and watched my husband nod his head and reply to her, but I couldn't hear the words. Darkness flowed through my mind, and my brain shut down.

Many years, I thought miserably. I have many years, but *how* many years? I silently wondered to myself.

"It's going to be fine, Kath," Ron said as he gently guided me to the elevator.

Questions no one could answer flooded my brain. Could I have done anything differently? Why couldn't I have caught this damn disease earlier? Stage 3? Seriously?

Cancer.

The word itself is like a death blow to your gut. You listen to the doctor tell you about what is going to happen, the operations (six or more but who's counting?), chemotherapy, radiation, but you really are not listening because inside you are screaming, WHY ME? I don't want to die yet!

Your brain literally shuts off, and you robotically leave the office.

Denial sets in.

Anger follows.

Life changes. Forever.

As we drove home, I began to mentally prepare myself for the challenge. Breast cancer took my mother at the age of fifty-eight, and it took my grandmother. My other grandmother had it as well, although that wasn't what killed her in the end. Would it take me, too?

I decided then and there that I would be the first to survive and thrive. This is *my* life, and I get to choose what happens.

Game on, cancer, I silently said to myself.

You might have won this battle, but I'm going to win the war.

The thought propelled me back up onto the rainbow. I wasn't there for very long, but I was *there*.

I snapped back to the present.

I did win the war, I thought to myself. The fact that I am still here proves it.

It's all about faith.

I put my fingers to the keys and began typing about faith.

CHAPTER FOURTEEN

Faith Is Hard

FAITH IS HARD.

Why? Mostly because it's hard to have faith in something you can't see, touch, or smell. I can feel it in my heart, but I can't see it, and I certainly can't touch it. It becomes especially hard when your brain is talking you out of something your heart is telling you to do.

Many years ago, Ron and I took our two sons to Maine to visit family. I remember it was a beautiful morning, and my two brothers decided that we should all climb a mountain. Easy for them to say; I wasn't in "mountain climbing" shape back in those days. Still, off we went, despite my griping. Due to two bad knees, Ron stayed behind.

The climb wasn't bad, and I soon found myself at the top. Since I'm terrified of heights, I stayed by the tree line where I was certain I would be safe. My family, however, had no fear whatsoever. They all eagerly walked onto the cliff.

Although it was beautiful up there, I found myself frozen in place. I was absolutely terrified and refused to leave the safety of the tree line. In fact, from where I was standing, I couldn't see beyond the first rock. It was like an infinity pool as I couldn't see what was beyond the first ledge. So from my perspective, it looked like my sons were standing right at the edge of the mountain. Of course, I panicked even more and started pleading with them to come back.

Actually, if you want me to be completely honest with you, I wasn't just pleading; I was yelling, like a screaming lunatic.

My brothers clearly agreed that I was a lunatic because they both turned around and looked at me like I had lost my mind.

To calm me down, my younger brother called to my sons to come back. He then turned around and started to walk toward me. When he got closer, he gently asked me to walk toward him and told me that it was completely safe. Come and see for yourself, he said.

Faith.

Having faith in something you can't see, and trust that my heart knew what it was doing.

My inner voice gently nudged me forward.

Shaking like a leaf, I took a step. Then after a deep breath, I took a few more. I soon found myself standing on a very flat rock that winded around the mountain like a staircase. There was no steep cliff. I'll admit that I felt a bit silly and gingerly wandered around for a few minutes. To their credit, neither of my brothers laughed, nor did I get the famous "I told you so" line. They simply smiled at me, shook their heads from side to side, and we moved on.

Now why am I telling you this story?

It's all about faith.

If you have hit a wall with your personal life (or career), then it's time to move beyond the clearing. You need to move beyond the safety of the trees so that you can go to the next level of your life.

Now, I completely understand that it's hard; I've been there. But you must move beyond those fears if you want to get beyond the tree line. Is it a fear of success or a fear of failure? What if I told you that you absolutely can't fail? Would you move forward? What would you do? How would you act? What's the first step you would take to make your dream a reality?

Do that now.

Know that there is a huge, flat rock beyond that clearing. You might not be able to see it from your vantage point, but it's there. Now take a deep breath and start. Let faith and your inner voice be your compass.

What's the worst thing that can happen? You'll fall? I've fallen thousands of times. There's absolutely nothing wrong with falling. It's only wrong if you don't pick yourself back up and try again.

Listen, if you are uneasy about something, or it just doesn't feel right, don't ignore that. Don't ignore uneasiness. Trust it. Have faith in your feelings. Don't let your brain talk you out of what your heart is telling you to do.

My inner guidance, my intuition, if you will, saved my life, and it could save yours. You can call this inner voice God or Tom, Dick, Harry, or Sue. I actually don't care what you call it. Just trust it. These warnings are like an alarm going off in your house. You know something is wrong. Search around to find out what it is. Don't ignore it.

Now take my hand and take that first step. I know you can do it.

If you have faith, you can do anything.

CHAPTER FIFTEEN

Game On, Cancer

RELIVING MY TIME IN THE cancer field was difficult. I stopped writing, reached for the glass of water on my desk, and took a long drink. As I held the glass, I leaned back in my chair and listened to the birds outside my office window.

Faith. It's incredibly hard to have faith when you are facing the worst banana peel of your life, I thought to myself. Cancer wasn't just a single banana peel; it was a whole field of the damn things. It took me two years to find my way out of this field. Although I managed to remain positive through it, it was the most difficult and darkest period of my life. Only my closest friends and family knew the truth of what I went through.

As I stared out the window and my mind wandered back to that blasted field, I barely noticed that it was a lovely sunny day. Waves of memories surfaced and threw me back in time again.

I landed in 2012 . . .

As promised, my surgeon fast-tracked me, and I was told to report to the hospital for a double mastectomy one week later.

It wasn't easy keeping my mind off of what was about to happen, but I stumbled through the rest of the week as best as I could. To keep from thinking about my cancer, I kept myself as busy as possible. Easy to do since I run a consulting business.

As luck would have it, I had a large, critical project that I absolutely needed to finish before the surgery, so I worked like a maniac to get it done. I muscled through fourteen-hour days, only stopping for meals and quick breaks. To everyone who spoke to me that week, it appeared as if I was taking everything in stride. Inside, however, I was screaming, scared out of my mind. Was I going to die from this disease? I had no answers, but I knew that "stinking thinking" was going to get me nowhere.

On the day of the surgery, my husband and I drove to the hospital. Not many words were spoken. He held my hand for most of the drive and continued to hold on to me as we walked into the hospital.

"If something happens during surgery," I began.

"You're going to be fine, Kath. You're not going anywhere," he said.

We checked in, and the nurse took us to pre-op where we waited for the surgeon. Ron gave me one last kiss, and then they wheeled me to the operating room.

When I woke up six hours later, I was in a hospital room. As I opened my eyes, I immediately looked for my husband, who was sitting in a chair next to my bed.

"Am I okay?" I asked Ron.

"You're fine. They got it all, Kath. It spread to three lymph nodes, but they took six and had to scrape your chest wall. You're completely cancer free!"

I smiled and lifted the sheets to look at my chest.

"Those are your expanders," he said. "They will stay there for at least a year."

"Why so long?"

"They can't give you your new girls until you've been finished with radiation for a year."

"That sucks," I answered. "This whole thing sucks."

"Yes, it does," he said.

"At least they're smaller than my real ones were. A small silver lining," I said. I had always wanted breast reduction surgery, but certainly *not* like this.

"I'll be the only one in the nursing home with perky boobs," I joked. "Everyone will be jealous."

He smiled and squeezed my hand as I slipped back into sleep.

I was in the hospital for more than a week. I remember people coming and going, but the morphine haze erased the details of who they were and what they said to me.

When I woke up again, I saw my friends George and Patty sitting next to my bed.

"Want some?" I cheerfully asked Patty.

"Want what?"

"Some of this." I raised the morphine pump and offered it to her. At least, I was a polite and happy drunk.

"No, thanks. I'm good," she laughed. "How are you feeling?"

"I'm doing okay. I love the balloon and flowers. Thank you so much," I said. I tried to keep my eyes open, but the morphine was pushing them closed again. As hard as I tried, I just couldn't stay awake or keep any thoughts in my head.

"Our pleasure. Go ahead and sleep. We'll be right here."

I smiled and slipped back into sleep.

When I came out of the drug haze a week later, I knew what I had to do—I had to fight to stay cancer free.

Cancer might have won this battle by taking my breasts, but I was going to win the war.

As Ron wheeled me to the car, I had the same thought again:

GAME ON, CANCER!

I paused, dropped my hands into my lap, and swung my chair around to look out the window.

Giving up would have been so much easier, I thought to myself. Two years of being sick was exhausting and *hard.*

Giving up is the easy way out. Too bad that I never take the easy way, I smiled to myself.

I returned to the keyboard and started tapping.

CHAPTER SIXTEEN

Giving Up Is Easy

GIVING UP IS EASY.

Seriously.

It takes no effort at all to just throw in the towel and walk away.

What is *not* easy is staying the course.

Rolling up your sleeves, taking a deep breath, and diving into that problem head first is *hard*.

I should know as I have personally shut down two companies and an association. Closing them was easy. Walking away is easy. Pulling the covers over your head is *easy*.

What is *not* easy is starting over and trying again until you get it right. I reformed both the association and my company and tried again and again—until I got it right.

Giving up is clearly not in my vocabulary.

It would have also been easy to give up on my cancer battle and go up to heaven, but that's not who I am. I'm a fighter who wins her battles, and I am winning that one.

Was it easy?

Nope.

Was it easy reforming my companies?

Of course not.

It was hard but so worth it. I am blessed.

Here's the reality: If you want to live your dream, then DON'T GIVE UP NO MATTER WHAT! Don't listen to people when they try to talk you out of your dream. Forget the ones who are telling you to shut it all down. Just ignore them.

This is *your* life, not theirs. You choose which roads to walk down and which ones to ignore.

Cancer has taught me many things, but one of them is this: Your life's path is yours to choose. No one can do it for you. Others can offer advice and comments, but at the end of the day, it's yours to win or lose.

As I said previously, studies show that only 10 percent of your success and happiness comes from outside sources. Only 10 percent! So clearly your life and business success is an inside job. It's a head trip.

It's all up to you.

That being said, I choose to win my battles. I choose to be happy and prosperous. I choose to live.

Sure, life will continue to throw hardballs at me. That's what life is all about. The "you know what" will hit the fan once in a while. How you get through that battle is all up to you. I might not be able to control the fact that I got cancer, or the fact that my company was brought to its knees. What I *can* control, however, is how I get through it. I can choose to fight and not give up. I can choose to start over and try again.

So stand up and fight.

Stand up and win.

Stand up and live your dream.

Just stand up and never, ever give up. No matter what.

CHAPTER SEVENTEEN

Mama Smeagol

AS I OPENED MY EYES, I happily realized that it was Sunday morning. I love Sundays. A nice easy morning drinking coffee, reading the paper, and watching Oprah's Super Soul Sunday. Perfect.

Since Ron was still sleeping, I closed the bedroom door quietly and walked downstairs to turn on the coffee and take our little dog outside. The cold hit me the minute I opened the backdoor.

Damn, it's cold today, I thought to myself.

Once back inside, I poured a cup of coffee, grabbed the newspaper, and headed for the family room to turn on the fireplace. I love our gas fireplace. Instant fire. The dog settled into her favorite spot on the couch while I sat and stared at the fire. The flames were mesmerizing. I watched them dance up and down and felt the heat start to warm up the room.

As I sipped my coffee, my mind started to wander back in time.

I can't believe that I am finally on the other side of that hell, I thought to myself.

As that thought snuggled into my mind, I settled deeper into the couch and allowed my memories to take me back . . . to July 2012. The month that I started a grueling course of chemotherapy.

It took several months to recover from the double mastectomy, but, eventually, I was able to resume a semi-normal life. Although the physical pain I experienced was met with pain medication, the mental pain was crushing me. Fighting off depression was a daily struggle.

It was impossible *not* to think about cancer and dying when they just cut off your breasts.

What would chemo and radiation be like? I frequently wondered. Inside I was scared out of my mind. To the outside world, however, I seemed to be taking everything in stride. I had learned quite young to never let them see you sweat, and it became my mantra. I tried to keep my mind positive by doing gratitude exercises every morning, listening to positive music, and keeping the people around me laughing. It helped.

Being positive wasn't easy on me, though. Truthfully, it was a daily challenge. A minute-by-minute choice that I had to make. Why bother? Mostly because it helped me push the demons to the back of my mind. Making people laugh and helping them with their problems became a welcome break from my illness and allowed me to forget that I was fighting a disease that might kill me.

I spent the next few weeks going from doctor to doctor. My life-saving surgeon needed to see me to follow up, and I had to regularly visit Dr. Karl Schwarz, my plastic surgeon (a great man who did an absolutely fabulous job). Although I looked like a plastic store mannequin now, eventually he was going to rebuild me and make me look a bit more normal. Since my old breasts had tried to kill me, I was eager to get healthy ones.

I loaded up on things that I would need during chemo: a wig (which I bought while I still had hair), turbans, and scarves. I visited online cancer forums and read all the advice that women were sharing. It both helped and scared the wits out of me.

Toward the end of July, I visited Dr. Neeraj R. Agrawal, my new oncologist, who was a very warm and friendly man, to talk about my treatment plan. I was facing six months of three different types of serious chemotherapy, a year of Herceptin treatments, five weeks of daily radiation, and at least five more operations.

Sigh.

Just thinking about it crushed my mind.

It was a sunny day in the first week of August when Ron and I found ourselves in chemotherapy class.

Yes, you read that right—chemotherapy class.

When we arrived at the cancer center, Rita, the earth angel at the front desk, cheerfully greeted us and signed us in. She was so incredibly warm and friendly it immediately made me feel better.

Perhaps this won't be so bad, I thought to myself.

As I walked into the conference room, I saw several other people already seated. No one smiled, and not a word was spoken. Ron and I said hello, and we quickly found a seat. My oldest son was with us, and he quietly headed to the chairs at the back of the room.

When the nurse walked in, she immediately started to talk about chemotherapy and what we could expect.

It was a grisly list with no positives in it at all. One by one, she listed the terrible things that would happen to me: loss of hair and possibly fingernails, massive pain, serious fatigue, nausea, memory loss, the list went on and on.

I was in the banana peel field up to my neck, and the peels were getting darker and darker.

The nurse made no mention of what I should be eating and doing; she just kept talking about the potentially bad side effects that I might get and needed to be aware of.

After about ten minutes, my brain rioted. I was sitting there listening, and then I wasn't. It was as if my mind just literally snapped in half.

Then I got angry.

No, I thought to myself. I won't do this. I won't get all these horrible side effects. Absolutely not.

I couldn't control the fact that I got cancer, but I could darn well control my perspective and my thoughts about it. So I decided then and there that I was *not* going to get all these nasty things.

And I didn't.

For the next six months, I got round after round of chemotherapy.

Since I was stage 3, the doctors hit me with everything they had. I lost my hair and my appetite and became a shadow of my former self. I was gaunt, pale, and unusually quiet. The pain, while mostly manageable, would often get intense. On those days, Ron and my two sons would just hold me in their arms. Not much else they could do for me.

Of course, since my family gets through pain by laughing about it, they teased me when I lost my hair, telling me that I looked like Smeagol from the movie *Lord of the Rings.* They called me "Mama Smeagol" for months.

It was a hard existence, but I got through it one day at a time. I ran my company from my bed on my laptop computer and kept my mind as positive as I could by listening to music, watching positive videos and movies, and laughing with my family.

The dog barking brought me back to the present with a jolt. Those days were behind me. When my mind cleared, I remembered that I was healthy now and enjoying a quiet Sunday morning by the fire. I didn't know how long I had been sitting there, but it was time to get up and run some errands. After a quick shower, I grabbed my keys and headed for the car.

When you don't feel well, and you don't feel like anyone's there for you, there's no reason to stop living your life. Friends may come and go, but your life does have meaning. Don't let other people control the meaning your life should have. If you don't like how you feel, how you look, or what life has given you, then think of it as a challenge that you have to conquer. If you face the challenge with no fear and full confidence, you'll conquer.

You have a choice. You can lie down and die if you can't face something, or you can get on with your life. The simple fact is that the problem/sickness is here. All you can do is face it. There is no reason to complain about what you have because there's a reason you got it in the first place and nothing will change that fact. It will change your life and make you a better person. It will make you the best of who you are and have ever been.

When life gives you problems, you shouldn't say, "Why couldn't someone else get this? Why do all the nice people get such bad things all the time?" The truth is it's not a bad thing unless you make it a bad thing. Your life's direction depends on your attitude toward the things that happen to you.

Everyone faces change in their life. It's really all about what you do with the change and your attitude toward it. If you can't accept it, you will never be able to be happy and move on because if you stay in your problems and pain you will never be able to get back to normal. So move on and accept the fact that your life is different now.

—WRITTEN BY JEREMY GIOVANNI IN 2013
AT THE AGE OF SEVENTEEN

CHAPTER EIGHTEEN

Jack Rabbits

UNFORTUNATELY, THERE ARE MANY DARK sides to being in a banana field, and one of them is this harsh reality: Some people around you will run. They might call once or twice, but they'll soon disappear as fast as a jack rabbit.

It doesn't matter why you are in the banana peel field. Whether you are sick, going through a divorce, or have a career or money crisis, the sad truth is that some people in your life will run.

I've always found it extremely interesting that when you are successful and riding that wave, everyone wants to be at your side. They all want to hitch their wagon to yours when you are at the top. However, when you fall and slip on a banana peel, or worse, and you find yourself in a *field* of the damn things, then they bolt like jack rabbits.

Why is that?

You know the story: When the team is winning, the stands are full. When the team is losing, the stands are empty—just when the team needs them the most.

Now here is the good news:

Your real family will actually run *to* your side, and they will stay there until you are out of the field and beyond.

Although I had a couple of jack rabbits (everyone does), I had dozens of people step up and help me, including my husband, Ron. For two years, he came to every single appointment, every surgery, every chemo infusion, and every radiation treatment. He cooked for me, cared for me, and became my lifeline. He was by my side every step of the way. Thanks are not enough. Words are not enough.

We also had friends, family, and neighbors step up. They made us dinner, sent e-cards, called me on the phone, came by and visited, sent goodies in the mail, texted me, and mailed beautiful cards. Others sent flowers, little gifts, and posted positive messages on Facebook. It was heartwarming and really helped me get through the dark days.

My husband is from Hoboken, New Jersey, and his family and friends were wonderful. I learned years ago that they stick together like glue and support each other no matter what. It didn't matter to them in the slightest that I didn't grow up there; I felt their love and support, and it helped get me through the cancer fields. Actually, it felt like the entire city of Hoboken had my back and was rooting for me. Their rally of "Jersey Strong" propelled me through many a dark, painful night. A truly great group of people.

Of course, to be completely authentic and fair here, I also had one or two jack rabbits.

One person called me up on the telephone and said that she saw my picture and the reason that she hadn't called me was because she didn't want to lie to me and tell me I looked great when I obviously didn't. So she decided to just not call at all.

Seriously?

What is wrong with calling me and saying, "You know, you really look like crap, but I wanted to call and see how you are feeling." Or just shoot me a text if you don't want to talk on the phone.

How about the woman who came up to me in a store when I was wearing my turban and said, "I am so sorry. How much time do you have left?" We'll overlook the pity looks that I got whenever I went out in public.

You just can't make this stuff up.

Then there were the people, bless their hearts, who told me they completely understood what I was going through because their mother, sister, cousin, aunt, friend *died* from breast cancer.

So not helpful.

Seriously, people, please do *not* tell a cancer patient about your relative who died from the disease. Conversely, if your friend is going through a huge drama, *don't* tell them you understand. Unless you have gone through it personally, you will not understand what they are going through.

Unbelievably, a few people actually asked me to come and visit *them*.

Really? My immune system wasn't working, and I was weak, bald, and sick from the chemotherapy, and you want me to drive to *you*?

Sigh.

Often I was too sick to talk, but I welcomed the distraction from my own troubles. I liked reading about what people were up to and chatting about normal things. The e-mails, texts, and calls really helped. If I was too sick to talk, I would either give the phone to Ron, or I would keep the call short and tell them I wasn't feeling well.

Why do jack rabbits leave? Hard to say actually.

First, there are the people who looked at me and remembered their mother/sister/aunt/grandmother who died from breast cancer. They ran because they just couldn't face it again.

Completely understandable.

Others looked at me and thought that if I could get cancer, then so could they, and it scared the wits out of them—so they ran.

Also totally understandable.

Then there were the people who were there in the beginning, but then after a few months bolted. Oddly, these people have disappeared on me, and I never heard from them again.

Ron and I actually used to wonder if people thought I was contagious.

I really don't think people bolt on purpose. I honestly think it's because they're not paying attention. It's not that they don't care; it's because their life swallows them up, and they just don't pay attention to anything outside of their own life.

And for the jack rabbits who ran because they *did* pay attention? Forgive them and let them go because you don't know what's going on in their life. Some people can handle it, and some people can't, so bless them and let them go. When you're healthy again, and they come back into your life, which some will, it is completely up to you whether or not you want to take them back into your life.

I learned that carrying bitterness and anger wouldn't help my recovery, so I practiced forgiveness (and still do). Carrying bitterness and anger is *not* going to help you become the new healthy you.

Let it go.

Cancer has taught me many other things as well, but a big lesson is this: I learned to be with people who celebrate me (and I celebrate them), and to avoid the ones who are just tolerating me. Life is just too short to be spending it with people who don't really care about you. Besides, it will be obvious who your family is because they will still be there when you get out of the banana peel field. Some probably walked through it with you.

At the end of the day, all we have is love. So I'm holding on to my dear family and letting the jack rabbits be. Life is precious. It's a gift not to be wasted.

Birthdays are not a guarantee; they are a gift.

Cherish every moment you are here.

Giving up is easy.

Change is hard.

That's why people run away from their friends. You see their struggle and the long road ahead of them, but then you see the backdoor so you slip out. It's easy. Slipping out is easy, but that selfishness will cost you a friend.

If you are running away, how many other people are running away, too?

Do you want to be known as "the person who ran away" or do you want to be known as the reason they got through it?

That's why I never run.

—WRITTEN BY MATTHEW GIOVANNI IN 2014
AT THE AGE OF TWENTY

CHAPTER NINETEEN

The Minute-by-Minute Job

IT HAD BEEN A HECTIC morning. I had a dozen e-mails and several voice mails to answer when I got to my office. After dispatching all the e-mails and finishing my calls, I finally got a chance to breathe and decided to work on my book. So I opened my file on my computer and randomly scanned the pieces I wrote when I was going through chemotherapy.

One in particular grabbed my eye, and as I opened it, I immediately remembered when I wrote it. It was the morning I had my first brain CT, and instead of watching television to distract myself, I wrote the following:

I am sitting alone in my house waiting for my husband to pick me up to get a brain CT. They scan me all the time now checking for cancer.

Thinking about your mortality is an interesting feeling. As I sit here, I wonder about it. You question everything.

Am I eating right?

Is the water pure or killing me?

Will a random chemical in my food bring it back?

If it comes back, is it my fault?

WILL it come back?

I have no answers, but I can tell you this: It's all up to you really.

I can't control the fact that I got cancer. Nor can I really control it, if it comes back. What I *can* control is my perspective. I can live my life with a positive attitude, knowing that I am doing all that I can.

On days like today, though, being positive is *hard*. It would be easier, I suspect, if I was watching TV or something to distract my mind but I'm not. I'm sitting here, writing in hopes that my thoughts will help you.

Is dying so bad?

Or is living the bad one?

Is heaven *real*?

I have no idea.

What does death even feel like? Is it like walking into a dream and staying there? Does it feel real?

Will I just vanish?

Fear creeps into my mind as that thought registers on my brain.

I push it back.

Cancer has taught me to live in the moment and enjoy being here today. Even on bad days like this one, I am still here with you. You're reading this, and the two of us are sharing a moment. Right now. Here. Together. So know that you are not alone. No matter what the doctors are telling you—YOU CAN DO THIS!

Sometimes being positive is a minute-by-minute job. You have to purposely shove the dark thoughts of impending death far into the back of your mind. Be careful because fear is easy. It creeps back into your brain in a flash and will stay there and grow if you let it. Being positive brings the light in. It bathes your mind with fresh thoughts of joy, life, and love. It heals.

Easy for me to say? Not right now it's not.

I'm sitting here alone in my kitchen waiting for my ride to the hospital. I don't want to drive due to the 50 milligrams of Benadryl I had to take.

So here I sit.

Waiting.

Thinking.

Fear creeps in.

I push it back.
It comes back again.
I watch a music video telling me to be brave.
Tears come.
I push thoughts of death away again.
Rinse and repeat.
Damn.

CHAPTER TWENTY

Don't Die Until You're Dead

I DON'T BELIEVE IN FAILURE.

Not because I never fail, but because failure usually gets me going in the right direction. So dying from this disease was not on my agenda. I simply refused to give up.

Don't die until you're dead, right?

Here's something else I don't believe in: I don't think you can be happy and positive 100 percent of the time. It's not sustainable. Why? Mostly because life has a nasty way of hitting you when you're not looking, and when it hits hard, it's usually not pretty. Hard to be positive when you're in crisis mode and feeling like hell.

So, here's something else I learned in my trip through the banana peel fields: It's okay to not be okay, just don't live there.

You need to pick yourself up, dust yourself off, learn from it, and move on. It really doesn't matter if you're talking about a business mistake or a life-altering moment, you still need to recover from it and move on. Dwelling on it will not make it go away. Trust me on this.

Dwelling on the fact that I got breast cancer did nothing except make me feel worse. It didn't cure me, nor did it make the pain go away. As I have said many times before in this book, I couldn't control the fact that I got cancer, but I darn well could control how I got through it. So I mentally decided to get through it with as much grace as possible.

I can't control what's happening to me on the outside, I can only control me on the inside. My perspective about the situation. I can trust that it's temporary and will eventually pass. I can focus on something better.

Now that I'm on the other side of cancer, I can safely tell you that looking at it from a positive perspective got me through with minimal side effects. Some days were harder than others, of course, and often I had to rely on other people to raise my spirits, but I'm still alive and darn proud of it.

Dwelling on the fact that some business ventures of ours failed did nothing to help the situation. It actually made it worse. If you keep looking at the bad side of something, eventually it will drag you down and you'll stay there. Admittedly, it's hard to be happy when you're looking at negativity and a bank account going in the wrong direction. Look at it this way, though—you didn't fail; you successfully learned what didn't work. Now go try again. Never give up.

No matter what.

Here's a reality check: If you want to be a success in both life and business, then you're going to fall down once in a while, and it's going to hurt. Life is like that. One day you are on top of the world, and the next day you're down on the ground. The trick is to look at the positive side of things when you're down there.

How do I stay positive when life hits me in the face? I laugh. Ron and I crack jokes and poke fun at the situation. We then look at what we *do* have and practice gratitude. We smile even when we don't feel like it, and we help other people be happy.

So, if you are facing a major business or life crisis, **it's okay to not be okay!**

It's perfectly fine to be upset or angry about it. Just remember, do not stay there because the longer you stay down in negativity, the harder it is to get up again.

Think of the banana peel field. The longer you stay in there, the darker the bananas will get. There's no light in there so you have to trust your instincts to get out. Trust me. Been there. Done that. Bought several T-shirts.

Being positive in a crisis is often a minute-by-minute choice. It's something you have to work hard at.

So when life throws you down on the ground and into the banana peel fields, keep getting up.

Follow your intuition and let it guide you. Your heart knows the way.

To help you along, I've created a twenty-one-day challenge that you can find in this book. It has exercises, tips, and worksheets to help you live a life that goes above and beyond anything that you can imagine.

CHAPTER TWENTY-ONE

The Longest Fifteen Months

WHAT A GREAT DAY FOR a drive, I thought to myself.

We were on our way home from my regular oncology appointment.

Thank God they didn't find any cancer, I thought to myself. What a blessing that I am still cancer free.

Since Ron was driving, I stared out the window daydreaming. Pretty soon my mind wandered back to the summer of 2012 when I started a grueling course of chemotherapy and Herceptin treatments that would last fifteen months.

It was a beautiful sunny day, but I wasn't paying a lick of attention to it. As Ron and I took the elevator to my oncologist's office, I was filled with determination and completely focused on the chemo drugs that were about to be pumped into me.

"It's going to be fine, Kath," Ron said, gently squeezing my hand.

"I know," I answered quietly. "Cancer sucks."

"Yes, yes, it does."

When we walked in, Rita cheerfully greeted us as I signed in. Quite soon we had her (and everyone else in the waiting room) laughing. It was the only way we could face this grim place—by making everyone around us laugh. It helped take our minds off of the pain.

A few minutes later we were shown into an exam room. Ron took his usual seat, and I hopped onto the table. When Melissa (my outstanding PA) arrived, we talked about my treatment and then cracked jokes. She left the room a few minutes later laughing hysterically.

"Maybe we should do stand-up?" I joked to Ron.

"Maybe. It's a thought." He smiled.

Since I had already lost my hair by that point, I straightened the turban on my head, and we headed to the chemo chair.

As I settled in with my book and iPhone, Ron tucked the warm blanket we brought with us around me. He then went to the break room to get me a snack and some water.

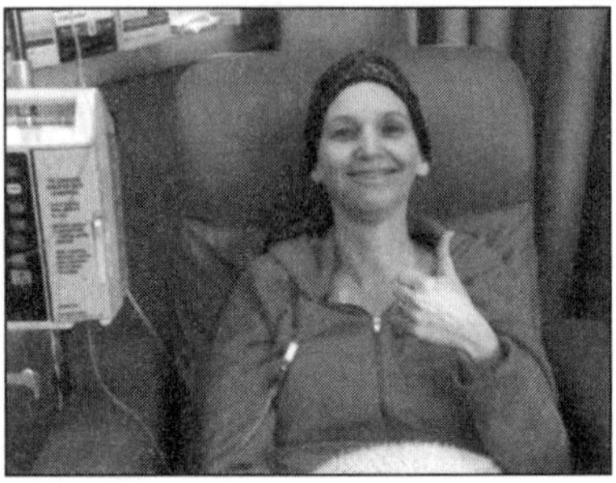

I imagined that the chemo drug was a life-healing liquid filled with love and light.

Life was challenging these days, as the chemo was really starting to work. Chemo is cumulative, which means the more you get, the sicker you feel. Certainly, that was the case with me.

As the nurse placed the first bag next to me, I closed my eyes and did my weekly meditation. I imagined that the chemo drug was a life-healing liquid filled with love and light. I then imagined that the liquid was flowing through every part of my body. As it flowed, it killed the dark cells that came across its path. After about five minutes, I opened my eyes and looked for Ron.

"Are you all right?" he asked.

"Absolutely. I'm fine," I said smiling.

Since the drugs made me really sleepy, a few minutes later I was fast asleep.

About fifteen months later, after dozens and dozens of treatments with various nasty drugs, chemo was finally over.

I was scary thin, in pain, and had little energy, but I was alive! The chemo had done its job well.

I snapped back to the present when Ron pulled into our driveway.

As I walked into the kitchen, my mind was still filled with memories of chemotherapy. Life was rough in those days. Since the drugs took potshots at my immune system, I rarely left my house and mostly lived on the couch with my laptop, the television, and some painkillers. What got me through was being positive and keeping my thoughts carefully centered on the fact that I was cured and would soon be back to my normal self.

Faith and hope, I thought to myself as I took the stairs to my office. That's what kept me going. Faith that I was going to live, and hope that I would never return to the days of chemo again.

Inspired, I began to write the minute I got to my desk.

CHAPTER TWENTY-TWO

Faith and Hope

FAITH AND HOPE.

Which one do you need right now to change your life?

Faith implies the "now." I have faith that something will happen.

Hope implies the future. I hope that something will happen. It's a destination.

Faith is confidence.

Hope is belief.

Personally, I believe that you need both faith and hope.

Faith is the confidence that what you hoped for came to pass.

Hope leads to faith.

Once you choose hope and faith, anything is possible. You can't have faith until you have hope. Start expecting great things to happen!

Now place your hand over your heart.

Feel that?

You're alive for a reason.

Never, ever give up.

CHAPTER TWENTY-THREE

What Is Your Birthday?

I WOKE UP, STRETCHED, AND went downstairs in search of coffee.

Once brewed, I took a cup and went to the couch and sat down with the newspaper. So many grisly headlines, I muttered to myself.

Then I saw an article on cancer. As I sat there, my mind went back to the last piece of my treatment: radiation.

I started radiation in 2013, and I remembered it like it was yesterday.

As we sat in the waiting room, my eyes scanned all the patients. Every generation was represented from old to young.

Cancer shows no mercy, I thought miserably.

After I met with the doctor, the nurse gently guided me back to the treatment room. It was a large and cold room with a huge round disc over the exam table.

I climbed on the table and lay down on my back. I'm not claustrophobic, but this was creepy.

I watched as the machine went back and forth over my body. It didn't hurt at all, but that red beam was freaking me out.

What if it zapped the wrong place? I silently wondered. The doctor told me it wouldn't, but I couldn't get the thought out of my head. I stayed as still as a stone while the beam went back and forth across my body. It certainly didn't help that I could hear a small hum when the darn thing turned on.

In desperation, I closed my eyes and started to daydream about a healthy body. I saw myself jogging again and writing a book about my experience. I then prayed and affirmed that I was in the pink of good health.

A few minutes later, the treatment was over, and Ron and I went home.

For the next six weeks, Ron and I made the daily trek to radiation. It was grueling, but soon we got used to it. I was tired, and my skin got really sore and red, but physically the treatments weren't too bad. It was certainly better than chemo! The beam still freaked me out, but I managed to keep my panic down by meditating and praying every time I was on that table.

On the tenth day, the nurse called my name and I soon had her laughing as we walked to the treatment room.

As I laid down on the table, she asked me her usual question, the same question she asked me every morning.

"What is your birthday, Mrs. Giovanni?" the nurse asked politely.

"May of 1951," I replied with a huge grin.

"Um, excuse me?"

She lifted her head up from the chart she was reading and gave me a penetrating stare.

"Yes, 1951," I replied firmly. "If you think I'm sixty-one right now, how great do I look?"

We both laughed.

"Quite right. Nineteen fifty-one it is then!" she replied smiling.

"Everyone always wants to go back ten years, I say you should go forward!" I said smiling broadly. If I had to go through this, I might as well laugh my through it.

"Now, hold still, this won't take too long." As she walked away, I could see her shaking her head and smiling.

For the rest of the treatments, I randomly changed my birth year. I also continued meditating every time I was on the table. Eventually, the radiation treatments came to an end.

I was tired, in pain, and sore as hell, but it was done. I still had a few months of Herceptin treatments, but I was getting closer to the finish line.

CHAPTER TWENTY-FOUR

The Caregiver's Path

BY RON GIOVANNI

MY FIRST DAY AS A caregiver began before the diagnosis. It started when Katharine found the lump. At first, I stayed positive because I did not want to worry her with my fears.

I had to be there for her: to hold her, to tell her I loved her, and to be a positive force no matter what the doctors said.

Really there was no time to be anything other than a loving husband, father, and caregiver. Yes, I still had to be a strong father for our two sons, but at the end of the day, all four of us were going to fight and support each other.

Once the official diagnosis was given, we had little time to process the news. Katharine's cancer was an aggressive one, and she was fast-tracked into surgery. We had to get rid of this cancer. Now. It was time for both of us to attack it together.

Yes, I said both because we were in it together, even though it was Katharine who had to fight it. We have always been partners, and this challenge was no different. I wanted her to know that I was with her every step of the way no matter what. My role was to be positive, to hold her hand and be there when she woke up from the surgeries. My role was to be present at every single doctor's appointment. Ours was a partnership, a friendship, and she, most importantly, was the love of my life. So nothing would pull me away from Katharine and her care. I made sure she got the care she needed to survive this.

Throughout this whole heart-wrenching time, I knew I was where I needed to be. I heard of many partners leaving once the other partner got sick—a thought that just boggles the mind. Incredibly, no matter what the relationship was, we heard of many people who just abandoned the one they said they loved. Love just doesn't get up and leave when something changes the direction of your life. You must stay and be part of it. In sickness *and* in health, right? I could not imagine not being the caretaker of my wife.

So, if you are ever called on to be a caregiver, here are my five top tips.

1. Be there, be strong, be funny, and love! Love them strongly and completely and make sure you take care of yourself, too.
2. Make sure that they know you are there for them always. Go with them to every appointment, no exceptions.
3. Stay positive no matter what happens.
4. Laugh! Always continue to laugh and joke. Laughter has amazing healing powers.
5. Hold onto your faith no matter what you believe in. Faith brings strength that you never knew you had.

We have come out on the good side of things so far, but we still keep our faith close by. We live with lots of love, and we live each day to the fullest.

Please remember, a caregiver is the most important job you can have outside of being a parent. Embrace it; do not run from it. You will feel fear, you will feel drained and tired, but you also will feel the most fulfilled as your loved one looks at you knowing that you are there for them.

Live, love, and laugh even when it seems to be the darkest.

CHAPTER TWENTY-FIVE

Real Estate in the Valley of the Shadow of Death

IT'S SO NICE TO BE able to do things again, I thought to myself.

I was in the kitchen baking cookies for my sons who were home for a break from college.

I took the cookies out of the oven and put them on the stove to cool.

Darn, they smell good, I thought to myself.

So I grabbed one and bit into it. As I chewed, I thought about cookies and how easily they crumble.

I don't crumble as easily, I thought, but I do eventually.

In an instant, my mind rolled back to January 2014 and a banana peel field waiting for me in a store fitting room.

My reconstruction surgery was getting closer, so I headed off to the store to buy a sports bra. Since my foobs (which stands for fake boobs) were going to be a smaller size, I needed to find something that would fit me.

Happily, I was finally able to drive myself places again. You have no idea how lovely it was to be able to drive myself around again. In the car, I turned the music up and sang to my favorite song all the way to the store. Once there, I found a parking space and went inside.

For about ten minutes, I walked around the lingerie section. Since I had no idea what size I was anymore, I randomly selected a few items and headed for the fitting room.

Life is filled with moments, and some moments are better than others. I'm actually really good at getting though a crisis and generally don't crumble until it's all over. I had been through two years of crap, and I never broke down once. Although I still had a few operations ahead of me, the treatments were all over and I was in the home stretch. My life was slowly getting back to normal.

Once I got into the fitting room, I removed my shirt and reached for the first item to try on. As I stared at my reflection in the mirror, it hit me like a brick to the face.

WHAM!

I look like a plastic mannequin that's been through a war, I thought miserably. I stared at my chest and tried to remember what it used to look like, and I failed. I just couldn't remember.

The enormity of what had happened to me hit me like a freight train, and I sank to my knees and cried. All the pain and anguish of the last year came out as I quietly cried my eyes out.

After a few minutes, I dug a tissue out of my purse and dried my eyes.

I can't go out there looking like I've been crying, I thought to myself.

After several minutes, I heaved myself off the floor with a big sigh and looked at my chest again.

I should be grateful that I'm standing here at all, I thought. At least I'm still alive.

I have walked through the valley of the shadow of death. Thank goodness, I didn't build a house there! I smiled to myself.

I grabbed my items and quietly left to find the cashier.

When the cookies were finished, I made some tea and went back to my office.

Perhaps it's time to discuss how to stay positive even when the "you know what" hits the fan. I pulled my keyboard toward me and began to write.

CHAPTER TWENTY-SIX

Tips for When the 'You Know What' Hits

SO HOW *DO* YOU STAY positive when the "you know what" hits the fan?

Not easy.

Many of you reading these words right now might be perfectly healthy, but you are going through other dramas. Other things are being thrown at your fan, and you have found yourself flat on your back in the middle of a banana peel field.

So what do you do *now*?

You could just give up, but giving up is probably not going to make it go away.

I refused to focus on what happened because it was in the past. It happened, and there was nothing I could do about it. Worrying about it would not fix it.

You can't control the past. You can only control the present. The "right now." Right now is the first moment of your new life. All we have is this moment right now.

"Just words, Katharine. What action steps can I take right now?"

Good question. Here are thirty-three tips to help you move forward right now.

1. SMILE. Right now as you read these words. Seriously. Smile whether you feel like it or not.
2. Practice forgiveness. Forgive yourself and the people you are angry at.
3. Think and say positive, forward-moving thoughts that include loving words such as certain, capable, and happy. Words are powerful. Avoid negative words because you can talk yourself in or out of anything.
4. Daydream about a successful outcome. Then write down (in the present tense) what it feels like now that you have achieved it. Yes, I know it hasn't happened yet. Humor me and just pretend for a minute that it did. How does that make you feel? Now, read this twice a day.
5. Look at the situation as your launching pad to something even greater.
6. Have gratitude. Write down what you are grateful for right now. Do this every day for the next week.
7. Dance. Listen to some positive, foot-stomping music and dance. Can't dance? Neither can I, but I do it anyway when I'm alone in my office. Let it all go!
8. Eat clean. Eat clean, unprocessed food as much as possible.
9. Sleep on it. Sometimes a problem looks completely different the next day. So, sleep on it and revisit it in the morning with a fresh perspective.
10. Find some positive people in your life and learn what they do to stay that way.
11. Look at the bright side. I'm really good at looking at the bright side of things. It might take me some time, but I always find a way to spin things in a positive direction, or at the very least find something to laugh about.

12. Act "as if." Act as if it has already happened. Act as if you are healthy again, have money in the bank, are in a happy, healthy relationship— whatever your dream is.

13. Focus on today. The past is over and done. Stop looking backwards. That's not where your future is. Focus on right now. What can you do right now, even if that is just getting a cup of hot tea and meditating quietly.

14. Change your words. Stop saying, "I can't" and "I won't." Give those negative sentiments the boot.

15. Go outside for a few minutes. The fresh air will do you good.

16. Pass it forward and do something nice for someone today.

17. Read an inspiring book or watch an inspiring movie.

18. Meditate right now as you read this. Breathe in slowly and then feel your breath going out. Concentrate on your breathing. Focus on it. Now just be for a few minutes and let your mind go.

19. Surround yourself with positive pictures and colors. Really look at your home. Do the pictures, colors, and knickknacks make you happy? Do they bring back good memories?

20. Share three positive things that happened to you today with a close family member or friend, or your dog! Do it every night.

21. Something bad happen? Purposely pick out the bright side of it. Can't? Then joke and laugh about it.

22. Exercise. Seriously, it will help your stress level. Try to get in at least fifteen minutes of exercise a day.

23. Go out with some friends and laugh.

24. Plan a fun trip. You don't have to actually go; just do the research and find the perfect vacation spot. Print out a picture and look at it every day. When money allows, take the trip.

25. Try to not complain about anything for one entire day. Try it!
26. Play your favorite song and crank it up! Sing along!
27. Look at old photos. The great memories will make you feel great
28. Stand in the sun for ten minutes. Trust me, it will make you feel great. Just remember the sunscreen.
29. Sit quietly and have a nice long chat with your Higher Power. Have a pad of paper nearby and write down the thoughts that come to your mind.
30. Go to YouTube and find a great video to watch. Something that makes you laugh and smile.
31. Fight! Focus on being proactive; don't wallow in self-pity. Don't say, "What did I do to deserve this?" Stand up and FIGHT.
32. Tonight just before you go to sleep, write down the most meaningful moment of your day. Do it every night for at least a week.
33. Praise a different person in your social network every day by e-mail, text, or phone.

So what actions are you taking to change your life? Are you doing research? Reading books? Taking classes? Traveling? Researching on the Internet? Invest in yourself at least thirty minutes a day and watch how your life will change.

Every new direction you walk starts in your mind. Eventually, your decision filters down to your body and becomes a reality. It all starts with a thought.

As I have said before many times, you cannot change what happened to you; you can only change your perspective about it. You can only change your attitude.

You can choose to stand up and fight!

GET OUT OF THAT BANANA PEEL FIELD!

You can choose, right now, to WIN!

Live for today. *Today* you are here.

Right now is the first moment of your new life. It all begins right now. All we have is this moment. So what are you choosing to do *right now*? How do you want this to play out?

So the doctors have given you bad news. You can either accept it and stay on the ground, or you can get up. You can choose to fight. Choose to be positive and live the rest of your life to the fullest. That's how you are going to get through this.

It's a bump in the road. It's a hiccup.

You now have a new normal. You are now 2.0!

I have a new normal.

I am proud to say that I am Katharine 2.0!

CHAPTER TWENTY-SEVEN

The Bird with the Broken Wing

IT WAS A BEAUTIFUL AUGUST morning in Hilton Head. We had just arrived for a vacation and were settling into our rented condo. We had decided to take a short vacation before my chemotherapy started as we were pretty sure it would be our last for a few years.

The second morning we were there, I took my morning coffee out onto the porch and sat down in a chair. As I sipped my coffee, I noticed a black crow with a broken wing in the backyard. It was hopping around the yard looking for food. I also noticed that it kept going to a bush at the back of the building.

It must have a nest in there, I thought to myself.

As the days passed, I saw the crow every morning. I'm an early riser and was up every morning bright and early.

So was the bird.

The amazing part of this story is who joined it every morning! Like clockwork, crows started to arrive. First one, then another. Soon about twenty were in the yard surrounding the bird. Every morning they arrived, stayed about an hour, and then left. They never missed a morning. One or two would linger as the others left, staying for at least another hour, and then fly off.

The crow had so many friends! How cool was that?

I abruptly stopped typing, still smiling at the memory of the crow and its friends.

It's so important to have a support team, I thought to myself.

Maybe I should write about that.

I began typing again.

CHAPTER TWENTY-EIGHT

Circle the Wagons

WHEN YOU ARE HURT OR going through a crisis, it's incredibly important that you have a support team. We could be talking about any kind of crisis: business, personal, spiritual, or relationship. At the end of the day, a crisis is a crisis. It doesn't really matter what topic we are talking about when you're hurt. Everyone needs a support team to help get through the hard times. Your friends and family need to circle the wagons around you.

The key is to surround yourself with people who are really positive.

Let's go farther. As motivational speaker Jim Rohn says, "You are the average of the five people you spend the most time with."

So who are you spending time with?

Think about it. Are the people you hang with positive or negative? Do they help you or do they just sit there?

If you spend time with negative people, eventually their thoughts and ideas will seep into your brain, and at some point, you will start to talk just like them. You won't be able to help it because it's who you are spending time with.

Peter Voogd sums it up perfectly in an article he wrote for *Entrepreneur* magazine. To paraphrase Voogd: You know how the story goes. If you spend enough time with a group of millionaires, you will be the next. If you spend time with people who are broke and unhappy, you will eventually become broke and unhappy as well. Your friends' beliefs will rub off on you, and your thoughts will merge into the crowd's consciousness.

So if you can't get away from these people, try and sprinkle some positive people in the mix. Spend more time with people who have a good attitude with life and less time with those who only see the negative. Once you decide to spend time with happier people, you start meeting happier people. It's funny how that works. You'll just start attracting these people to you.

You can also show these negative Nellies how they could be living. Be the person who shines that light. Because the more time they spend with happy people, the happier they will be.

Remember the last time you bought (or wanted to buy) a car? Most likely you started to research the type of car you wanted. You probably also started paying attention to the cars on the road and noted what colors you like or didn't like. Yesterday, when you weren't looking for a car, you didn't pay attention to the cars on the road at all, right? Today, however, you are paying attention, and you're noticing every single car on the road and what they look like. This is the same thing. Once you make the choice to spend time with happier people, you'll start to actually pay attention and you'll start to see the happier people around you.

The trick to getting through a crisis is this: First, acknowledge the pain and the fear. Then get up and face it head on. Keep your focus on the future. Keep your focus on where you want to be—not where you are. Keep your focus on how *you* want this to play out.

Everything you want is on the other side of fear.

CHAPTER TWENTY-NINE

A New Normal

IT WAS A RAINY MORNING. I was in my office reading people's posts on Facebook when I saw a post on fighting cancer.

I leaned back in my chair and thought about the last two years.

Thank God, *that's* over, I thought to myself. The fight was *hard*. Horrible. It had been over a year since I was in chemotherapy, and life was slowly getting back to normal.

Getting my health back after the grueling cancer treatments was rough, but I was determined to get it back, despite what the doctors told me.

They said that I would not get back to 100 percent, that I would have a new normal, a new way of living.

Of course, telling me I can't do something has always been a huge motivator for me. They were fighting words.

Watch me, I remember thinking to myself. Challenge accepted!

So after treatments were over, I got on my treadmill six times a week. After about a month, I was able to start jogging again. I ate clean, organic food; drank a green smoothie every morning; and cut out as many chemicals from my environment as I could.

As the months went by, I slowly started to feel better.

I also listened to positive music. It inspired me and helped lift me when I was down.

Perhaps I should share my song list, I thought to myself. The songs really got me through some very dark days.

I really was Katharine 2.0 now!

I bent over the keys of my computer and started making my playlist.

CHAPTER THIRTY

Katharine's Positive Life Playlist

DID YOU KNOW THAT SOME recent research says that listening to music improves memory, strengthens your immune system, and reduces depression?

It also inspires me and lifts me out of a bad mood.

When I need inspiration to do something, I turn to music. It gets me back to that positive place so that I can do what I need to do. I recently put together a short playlist of upbeat music that inspires me. I listen to it when I am exercising or working at my desk. I actually have it on now as I write this. They're all upbeat, positive "pop" tunes that you can easily find on the Internet.

I also listen to it when I'm on my treadmill. Often, I'll put the playlist on, hit shuffle on my iPhone, and then say a little prayer asking God and the angels to give me messages through the songs. I'll then pay a *lot* of attention to the song messages as they randomly play on my phone. It's a spiritual rainbow moment I share with God every morning.

Please know that there are thousands of songs out there that will motivate you, so needless to say this is not a complete list. Here are one hundred of my favorites in alphabetical order by artist.

1. "Just a Prayer Away"—Yolanda Adams
2. "Beautiful"—Christina Aguilera

3. "Fighter"—Christina Aguilera
4. "Beautiful"—Akon
5. "Heroes (We Could Be)"—Alesso
6. "Get It Together"—India Arie
7. "What a Wonderful World"—Louis Armstrong
8. "Best Day of My Life"—American Authors
9. "Brave"—Sara Bareillles
10. "All You Need Is Love"—The Beatles
11. "Here Comes the Sun"—The Beatles
12. "Pocketful of Sunshine"—Natasha Bedingfield
13. "Unwritten"—Natasha Bedingfield
14. "I Gotta Feeling"—Black Eyed Peas
15. "Heroes"—David Bowie
16. "I Feel Good"—James Brown
17. "Through the Rain"—Mariah Carey
18. "Hero"—Mariah Carey
19. "When You Believe"—Mariah Carey and Whitney Houston
20. "Woman's World"—Cher
21. "You Haven't Seen the Last of Me"—Cher
22. "Tubthumping"—Chumbawamba
23. "Change the World"—Eric Clapton
24. "Stronger"—Kelly Clarkson
25. "A Sky Full of Stars"—Coldplay
26. "Fix Me"—Coldplay
27. "Magic"—Coldplay
28. "Paradise"—Coldplay
29. "The Climb"—Miley Cyrus
30. "Start of Something Good"—Daughtry
31. "Be"—Neil Diamond, *Jonathan Livingston Seagull* soundtrack

32. "Lose Yourself"—Eminem (*some strong language*)
33. "Return to Innocence"—Enigma
34. "Stand"—Rascal Flatts
35. "Carry On"—Fun
36. "Don't Give Up"—Peter Gabriel
37. "Born This Way"—Lady Gaga
38. "I Will Survive"—Gloria Gaynor
39. "You Raise Me Up"—Josh Groban
40. "Lovers on the Sun"—David Guetta
41. "Titanium"—David Guetta and Sia
42. "Let's Go"—Calvin Harris
43. "I Didn't Know My Own Strength"—Whitney Houston
44. "It's Time"—Imagine Dragons
45. "Beat It"—Michael Jackson
46. "Heal the World"—Michael Jackson
47. "Man in the Mirror"—Michael Jackson
48. "Masterpiece"—Jessie J
49. "Who You Are"—Jessie J
50. "I'm Still Standing"—Elton John
51. "Don't Stop Believing"—Journey
52. "It's My Life"—Bon Jovi
53. "Testify to Love"—Wynonna Judd
54. "Somewhere Over the Rainbow"—Israel Kamakawiwo'ole
55. "Walking on Sunshine"—Katrina & the Waves
56. "I Believe I Can Fly"—R. Kelly
57. "Come with Me Now"—Kongos
58. "No Boundaries"—Adam Lambert
59. "Time for Miracles"—Adam Lambert
60. "True Colors"—Cyndi Lauper

61. "Keep Holding On"—Avril Lavigne
62. "Imagine"—John Lennon
63. "Skyscraper"—Demi Lovato
64. "Beautiful"—Mali Music
65. "Overcomer"—Mandisa
66. "Stronger"—Mandisa
67. "Just the Way You Are"—Bruno Mars
68. "How Great Is Your Mercy"—Donnie McClurkin
69. "Don't Worry, Be Happy"—Bobby McFerrin
70. "Live Like You Were Dying"—Tim McGraw
71. "Angels"—Sarah McLachlan
72. "Believe"—Suzie McNeil
73. "Let It Go"—Idina Menzel
74. "I Can Only Imagine"—Mercy Me
75. "I Won't Give Up"—Jason Mraz
76. "I Can See Clearly Now"—Johnny Nash
77. "You Get What You Give"—New Radicals
78. "What Are You Waiting For?"—Nickelback
79. "By the Grace of God"—Katy Perry
80. "Firework"—Katy Perry
81. "Roar"—Katy Perry
82. "I Won't Back Down"—Tom Petty
83. "Home"—Phillip Phillips
84. "Perfect"—Pink
85. "Diamonds"—Rihanna
86. "Towards the Sun"—Rihanna
87. "Follow the Sun"—Xavier Rudd
88. "We Are Family"—Sister Sledge
89. "One Step at a Time"—Jordin Sparks

90. “Born to Run”—Bruce Springsteen
91. “Eye of the Tiger”—Survivor
92. “We Are the Champions”—Survivor
93. “Dare You to Move”—Switchfoot
94. “This Is Your Life”—Switchfoot
95. “The Best”—Tina Turner
96. “Beautiful Day”—U2
97. “Something in the Water”—Carrie Underwood
98. “God Loves You”—Jaci Velasquez
99. “Happy”—Pharrell Williams
100. “Never Leave the Sun”—Yanni Voices

If you wish to listen to the playlist, my son Matt has created a playlist for you on Spotify. Songs are always being added. Here's the link: http://open.spotify.com/user/12100346637/playlist/7twj7jrC2SwddiNkIjFpEC

CHAPTER THIRTY-ONE

New Directions

I STOPPED TYPING.

Katharine 2.0 is right, I thought to myself. Everything in my life had changed. Health, diet, career, friends, everything.

Wish I had known all of this before I got cancer, I thought, as I walked downstairs to make my Giambotta Smoothie.

Why do you have to go through the black banana peel fields to transform your life? Why couldn't God have just *told* me all this?

Maybe He did and I wasn't listening.

I'll listen to you *now*, God, I thought to myself. I don't need to go through something like *that* again.

When I arrived in my kitchen, I bent down and retrieved my Ninja Blender. I just loved that thing.

I then opened the refrigerator and pulled out spinach, bok choy, celery, carrots, a beet, some frozen strawberries, unsweetened coconut milk, and some parsley.

I need to go to the store and change up my greens, I thought as I placed the food on the island. Although spinach was a staple, I often changed the dark leafy greens and frequently used kale, Swiss chard, and other greens. Every week was different and really depended on what vegetables were fresh in the store that week.

I quickly washed the vegetables and berries, chopped the vegetables, and threw everything into the blender. I then added a banana and chopped an apple to add to the mix.

The last thing that went in was the coconut milk and a little fresh ginger root and some fresh turmeric. Sometimes I used the powder when I didn't have the fresh roots on hand.

As I chopped the orange turmeric, I quietly blessed the ingredients in the smoothie. I knew the raw vegetables were helping me stay healthy, plus I felt better when I drank them.

The whole thing took less than ten minutes.

After it was blended, I divided the mixture into two glasses and wandered into Ron's office.

"It's your favorite time of day," I brightly said as I walked in and handed him the drink.

"Uh-huh," he grumbled.

"You know it makes you feel better."

"It does actually," he answered. He then downed the drink and handed me the empty glass.

Laughing, I bent down and kissed him, took the glass, and returned to the kitchen. A few minutes later, I was back in my office typing.

(*The recipe for my Giambotta Smoothie is in the resource section at the back of this book.*)

CHAPTER THIRTY-TWO

You Really Are What You Eat

PART OF LIVING A POSITIVE life and staying on that rainbow includes eating healthy and limiting your exposure to chemicals and processed food as much as possible. For normal people, this just makes good sense, but for me and many other people, it's a survival tactic.

So what should we be eating and drinking to avoid disease?

The research is mixed. In fact, when I was doing the research for this chapter, I almost went mad.

Be a vegetarian.

Don't be a vegetarian.

Detox.

Don't detox.

Take vitamins.

Don't take vitamins.

Eat this.

Absolutely do not eat that!

Go on the Budwig Diet.

No the macrobiotic diet is what you need.

AAHHH!

I also watched several documentaries in my search for the truth including *Food Matters* and *Forks over Knives*. Both of which I just loved.

However, for every fact/suggestion, there is someone else telling me that it is simply not true.

Back in the 1970s, my mother used to tell me that if researchers injected enough chocolate into a laboratory rat, then it would get cancer, which would lead to us all being told that chocolate causes cancer and we should not eat it.

She was not entirely wrong.

Furthermore, if you are sick and not feeling well, it's going to be *really* hard to be positive. Trust me on this one. It's hard being cheerful and optimistic when you are in pain. Negativity easily crept in when I didn't feel well, and keeping depression away and feeling sorry for myself was a daily battle.

So, I distracted myself and started searching the Internet for what I should be eating and drinking to keep cancer away for good. Eventually, I stumbled on to the clean eating philosophy.

Clean eating means exactly what you think it means. Eating healthy food that contain no chemicals and is not processed. It also means eating food that is good for the planet, food that is grown without pesticides, chemicals, or antibiotics. Genetically modified food (GMO) is also to be avoided.

Plus you might even lose a few pounds.

The trick to persuading your family to eat and live this way is to change over to this lifestyle *slowly*. I did it over the course of about nine months. We started with one vegetarian meal a week. I then changed our milk and eggs to organic. A few weeks later I added my Giambotta Smoothies (the recipe is in the resource section at the back of this book).

I also swapped out the commercial air fresheners in each bathroom to Myers (a nice organic brand), and my family loved them. Not only did they smell better, but they lasted longer than the commercial brands so it saved us money. All good.

Since I could write an entire book on this topic (and I might one day), I'm only going to give you a few tips here to get you going. The Internet is filled with websites, books, and articles that will teach you how to eat clean.

So what did my research find?

I discovered that information on what we should be eating and drinking is all over the place. Being a cancer survivor, my immune system has already been compromised, so to survive, I *have* to eat and live clean, but do you?

Probably.

Studies across the board all point to the same fact: A chemical-free diet high in fruits and vegetables is the healthiest. In fact, a science review by the World Cancer Research Fund and the American Cancer Institute for Cancer Research states that many veggies fight cancer.

That being said, I humbly suggest that you try to eat clean 75–80 percent of the time. Don't beat yourself up if you can't. If you can only eat clean 25 percent of the time, that's a great start. I fully understand that eating this way can be expensive, so just do the best that you can. The goal is to move forward and make changes gradually.

So, here are some health tips that worked for me. Please be aware that I do not have a medical degree, these are merely tips that I developed through this experience and found to work for me personally.

- I don't eat food that can be purchased through my car window.
- I eat low human-intervention food. How many people messed with it before it got to your table? What was it sprayed with? How old is it?
- I don't eat processed food, especially high fructose corn syrup.
- If I don't understand a word on the label, I don't eat it.
- I eat in more than I eat out.
- I make things from scratch. This way you control the ingredients.
- I either air pop popcorn, or I use a little oil in a pan and pop the old-fashioned way. There are way too many chemicals in the microwave bags. Google it. You'll stop using them, too.
- I eat NO GMOs (genetically modified organisms), if I can help it.

- I *never* put plastic in the microwave because the heat causes toxic chemicals to leak into the food. Only use glass. We actually have eliminated almost all of the plastic in our home.
- I never drink soda or energy drinks. I stick to water, tea, coffee in the morning, and fruit-infused filtered water. I know I should give up coffee, but life is short.
- I drink a green smoothie every day. My recipe is in the back of this book
- I avoid shredded cheese. Why? Food manufacturers use wood dust in shredded cheese to keep the cheese from sticking. Shredding cheese yourself is really easy.
- I use organic air fresheners and cleaners
- I READ LABELS!
- I try to cut down my sugar intake as much as I can. Never use artificial sweeteners.
- I try to not use artificial anything.
- If it says "natural," I don't buy it. Natural can mean anything from nature, meaning you could be ingesting beaver butt. (According to Snopes.com, it's called "Castoreum, a secretion produced by beavers that is used as a food additive.")
- I use organic shampoo and hair dyes that don't have parabens, propylene glycol, betaines, cocamide DEA, or sulfates. My hairdresser uses "All-Nutrient" products (http://www.all-nutrientorganics.com).
- I avoid fluoride and am currently using Tom's of Maine Toothpaste with no added fluoride.
- I also use organic makeup, moisturizer, soap, and perfume.
- I try to exercise six days a week. I suggest you do something that

you enjoy. Start slow and work your way up. Just try to do *something* thirty minutes a day.

- Bodum coffee—I use as much glass as possible, including storage containers. I avoid plastic. As I said before, when plastic is heated up, the chemicals in plastic leak into the food.
- I don't eat pork. When I eat chicken or fish, I eat organic, free range, with no antibiotics or hormones. Since I am a breast cancer survivor who cannot have added hormones, this is critical for me personally. As for red meat, I rarely eat it. Perhaps twice a year if that. As I said before, when I do eat it, it has to be completely organic, grass fed, no hormones or antibiotics. As clean as possible. When I eat at a restaurant, I choose vegetarian or vegan.
- I avoid food containing food dyes "Not only are food dyes causing hyperactivity, inability to concentrate, aggressiveness, sleep problems, increased symptoms of autism, and ADHD, among many others, but they are known carcinogens. They cause cancer."—*Seeing Red: One Mother (A Medical Writer) Investigates Food Dyes* by Amy Kilgore.
- I eat clean food, mostly fruits, vegetables, and whole grains.

Now, I completely understand that this new way of eating is inconvenient. You are busy. Some of you have kids, and you are running in ten directions at once. Drama finds you, and you are in crisis management most of the time.

I get that.

I did that! I have two sons and was crazy busy for years.

Then I got cancer.

It changes you, and you realize that death *can* find you.

With no warning, I might add.

So why wait to be happy and healthy? If you feel good, you will look better and be more able to handle the drama around you.

Happiness is *not* a destination. It's a feeling.

So make changes.

Limit your exposure to toxic things, and, yes, that means toxic friends and family. You already know who I am talking about as you read these words, right? Yes, them. Surround yourself with positive people who encourage you.

Start practicing gratitude so you can learn to be happy and grateful for what you have and stop beating yourself up for what you don't have.

Put down your glass of anger and resentment.

Eat clean and eliminate chemicals from your life.

Exercise. Do some type of exercise at least three to four times a week (or more) for thirty minutes. Take a walk. Park your car as far from the store as possible. Choose the stairs instead of the elevator. Stand instead of sit. Little things like this count. Just start doing something.

Of course, you could also try my GAAB Life 21-Day Challenge. GAAB stands for Going Above and Beyond. We go above and beyond for our clients and customers, why not go above and beyond for *yourself*?

Want the details? Keep reading. It is in an upcoming chapter.

CHAPTER THIRTY-THREE

Pitiful or Powerful?

THE PHONE ON MY DESK rang suddenly, jarring me out of my writing haze.

"Good morning, this is Katharine. May I help you?" I automatically answered.

"Hey, Kath, it's Linda."

"Linda, so nice to hear from you." It was a client of mine whom I hadn't heard from in a few months. "What's up?" I asked politely. There was something in her voice that made me sit up straight in my chair.

"I'm angry actually. I can't seem to stop being bitter about my family. I know you told me that anger is toxic, but I can't seem to move on," she said.

"Perhaps telling you how I handle this will help," I said. "I don't use what happened to me as an excuse to be bitter. That will just make me miserable. I let myself be angry for a while, and then I just decide one day to get over it and move on. If you don't, bitterness will move into your house. Hard to get rid of it once it takes root. A wise man once said, 'You can be pitiful or powerful but not both.' Harsh, I know, but true."

"That's not harsh. I needed to hear you say that. I *am* being pitiful."

"So many people blame the past for their current situation," I said. "Okay, so it was horrible, try and learn from this and forgive them.

Even though it was clearly not good enough, your family did the best they could. Don't be bitter and resentful. Blame and self-pity are easy. It's easy to remember what you didn't get. It's easy to remember what they didn't do for you. Why not show them how to do it right? Be a lighthouse for them to follow."

"You are absolutely right," she said in a small voice. I swear I could hear the tears falling down her cheeks through the phone.

"I know I'm on my soapbox, but anger and resentment is going to hurt you and make you sick. Here's the thing: You remember what happened, or you see their face on Facebook or somewhere and get angry again, right? But who are you hurting? The person you're mad at probably doesn't even know you're angry at him or her. So that person is living his or her life oblivious to the fact that you are totally miserable. So your anger only hurts you. It poisons you from the inside out. 'If only this hadn't happened to me,' you say. 'I could be . . .' Get rid of the 'if only.' Move on from it."

She started crying quietly into the phone.

"I know this is upsetting," I said.

"I'm not crying about that. I'm crying because you're right, and I feel like a weight is being lifted off my shoulders."

"Great! Are you still worried about money or did you land that job you were applying for?"

"I didn't get it, so the quick answer is yes I am worried now more than ever."

"I'm so sorry."

"It's okay. I'll find something soon."

"Well, in the meantime, perhaps I can help. To find your new job, trust your gut. Seriously, feel your way through this. It will help."

"I do trust my intuition, but I also worry. What if I can't get a new job? Then what will I do?"

"Let me word it this way. If you worry about something you want, you actually push it away. You're focusing on the lack—the not having—the 'I don't have a job' worry, the 'I'm sick and I don't know what to do' worry. You get frustrated; you worry more; you start to panic; that makes it worse.

"It's like swimming—if you get caught in a rip tide and panic, you'll drown. If you keep your head about you, then you float and can swim adjacent to the shore and work your way back to the beach. I suggest that you focus on what is going right in your life. Focus on the things you are grateful for right now."

"Hmm, I never thought of it that way," she answered.

"Did you know that many of your thoughts are programmed by the people who raised you? The good news is that you can reprogram yourself. You can retrain your brain. You can get rid of the 'You'll never amount to anything' thoughts. The 'You are stupid/fat/ugly/slow' thoughts. Instead, they should be saying how talented and great you are! You have greatness in you. Get rid of those old thoughts and become who you really are. I see a unique person with talent. I see the champion. I do *not see* nor do I believe in failure."

"Thanks, Kath, I appreciate that," she said quietly.

"Now that I am on the other side of cancer, I live in the moment. I practice gratitude and affirm that all is well in my life. I'm grateful that I have a house to live in, food to eat, and money to pay my bills. I was grateful for all these things even when I didn't have them. I acted 'as if' for years. Let me ask you an important question, do you feel worthy for great things to happen to you?"

"Not really."

"You should. You are a *great* person and totally deserve the best that life has to offer and more. You *are* worthy. Keep saying, 'I am worthy,' until you believe it. I believe in you!"

"Thanks, Kath. I really needed to hear that today."

When I hung up the phone a few minutes later, I thought about what I had just told her.

So many people have trouble with this. The idea that they are not worthy enough to have money or be happy. If you don't feel worthy enough to be happy, then all the affirmations in the world aren't going to help you. I also know a few people who would love to have a ton of money, yet they seriously think that all rich people are bad. Don't those two thoughts cancel each other out?

The first part of the journey to happiness involves knowing that you are worthy enough to live the life of your dreams. You have to feel like you deserve to be prosperous and happy, or it won't work. The fear will push it all away.

Choosing to *be* happy and then accepting the fact that you can be happy is a great place to start.

I'm so happy that I could help Linda, I thought to myself. I had learned that sometimes *you* have to be a rainbow for someone. You have to be their blessing. Their way out. The answer.

I picked up my keyboard again and began to write. Perhaps my twenty-one-day challenge will help Linda, I thought.

I bent over the keys, took a sip of my tea, and began to type again.

CHAPTER THIRTY-FOUR

Katharine's GAAB Life 21-Day Challenge

(To help you stop slipping on those darn banana peels!)

YOU GO ABOVE AND BEYOND for your family, friends, and customers/clients so why not go above and beyond for yourself?

GAAB Life = Going Above And Beyond to create a happy life!

Are you serious about changing your life?

Would you like to live in joy and peace?

Need to figure out how to be positive instead of negative and begin attracting *great* things into your life?

Have an illness?

Sick and tired of being sick and tired?

It really doesn't matter why you've reached this page in this book. By reading the words on this page, you are clearly ready to change your life.

One note of caution: I *slowly* changed my family over to this lifestyle over the course of about nine months. Although I began living this way pretty darn quick since I'm a cancer survivor, this lifestyle is really hard on people who are used to processed food, negativity, and fear.

I suggest you do the following program for seven days. THEN if you think you can keep it up, try it for another seven days and then another seven. Remember the old fable about the tortoise and the hare? Well, the darn tortoise won. So, clearly slow and steady wins the race. If you can only do one week, that's fine. Just start slowly adding in pieces of clean living one thing at a time.

WHEN TO DO THIS PROGRAM AND WHAT TO EXPECT

Try and pick a period of time when you have no weddings or special functions. It's much easier to do this program if you don't have to go to a special occasion where temptation will be lurking around every corner.

This challenge has three parts to it: body, mind, and spirit. So you will be detoxing all three for the next three weeks. You will detox your body of all those nasty chemicals, you will cleanse your mind of old anger and resentments that no longer serve you, and you will cleanse your spirit to get everything moving in the right direction.

After a few days, you might experience some side effects. You might get really tired, or get a headache (especially if you decide to give up caffeine, which many people do). Sleeping is your body's way of healing itself, so be good to yourself and allow your body and mind to heal. Rest. You might also be a bit more emotional than usual as you release anger and resentment from your body. Allow this and let it go, although you might want to warn your family about the potential for some emotional outbursts.

Feel the memories, then thank them for the lesson and let the feeling go. Personally, when I did these exercises, I allowed myself to cry and get angry. Then I looked at the person again in my mind and tried to see the person as a "teacher." Easy for some, *really* hard for others (smile). I then thanked the person for teaching me what not to do, or I thanked him or her for pushing me in a new direction. If I didn't know what the darn lesson was (and this happened once or twice), I just blindly thanked my teacher. Allow all the memories to come out. This is your brain's way of cleansing itself. Just make sure you drink *lots* of water to flush it all out.

The good news is that great things will start to happen to you. Your outlook on life will become more positive, and you will start to physically feel better. You might even shed a few pounds. Don't be surprised if some of the more negative friends/family/associates start to leave your life. That happened to me, and although it hurt like hell at the time, it really was for the best. The upside is that you will start to attract more positive, forward-thinking people into your life who will support you (versus sabotaging you).

Also, forgiveness is *powerful.* When I did the forgiveness piece, magical things started happening to me. My business worked better, more clients started to arrive, and money began to flow into my bank account. I saw the world a little more clearly and was able to put my mind to new things, like writing a new book, for example. It's hard to do things when you are angry and totally focused on the hurt. Once you let that all go, you suddenly have time on your hands. Your brain now has space to think, and new ideas start to flow. Great ideas! Write them down in a notebook as they appear so you can go back and revisit them to see if you wish to implement some of them.

Now please understand this process is not permanent because life ebbs and flows and stuff happens. Not to be a negative Nelly, but I guarantee you that eventually the "you know what" will hit the fan again, and you'll find yourself back in that darn banana peel field. I did the forgiveness exercise years ago, and it was so wonderful. Really helped me. Company started doing great; new friends appeared; life was good. Then out of nowhere— WHAM! Cancer happened. Back into the banana peel field I went, and I stayed there for two years. When I was finished with treatment, operations, and all the sickness, I did the exercises I've given to you in this chapter again, and everything started to flow as I started to feel better and better. Although I've been eating clean for years, there is always something cleaner you can add to your environment as new technology and information becomes available.

Please understand that this is not an instant overnight success; it's going take some time and work, which is why I call it a "challenge" because it really is quite challenging. If you are looking for a quick fix to use as a band-aid for your life's problems, this challenge is not it. Keep at it, though, and you'll be able to get out of your banana peel field.

Think of this challenge as your flashlight. It will help give you the tools you need to escape your banana peel field.

If you would like more information about how your body might react, here's a great article: http://www.incrediblesmoothies.com/detox/common-detox-symptoms-and-what-they-really-mean/

Now, I'm not a doctor. I'm simply a stage 3 breast cancer survivor who wanted to change her life. Below is the diet and lifestyle that works for me.

1. Eat clean for twenty-one days (or just start with seven days in a row).
2. Do the anger exercise for seven days, and then do the gratitude exercise.
3. Exercise and meditate.

You'll find one day's worth of worksheets at the end of this book. If you want the entire twenty-one days of worksheets, please just visit my website at www.katharinegiovanni.com.

CLEAN FOOD

The first worksheet is a "clean food log." I understand that you are busy, and processed food is quick and inexpensive, but getting sick is even more expensive.

As always, you should consult your doctor before you start any program that impacts your diet and nutritional needs.

Also, don't worry if you can't eat clean 100 percent of the time. I know it's hard. If you eat clean at least 75 percent of the time, I think that is a win! When you buy food in a box, bag, or package, read the label and try and buy food with as few ingredients in them as possible.

WHAT TO AVOID (YOU CAN DO THIS)

- Cigarettes, alcohol, recreational drugs *(yes, I had to go there)*
- Processed food

- No red meat or pork (unless it is organic, but still try to limit it if you can)
- Fast food
- Your microwave
- Hydrogenated oil
- Fluoride in your toothpaste *(yes, that is a chemical)*
- Refined sugar, artificial sweeteners, and any food that includes them on the label
- White flour and food that includes it
- Food that comes in a box, can, or a frozen dinner; any meal or food that is prepackaged or ready made
- Soft drinks, including regular and diet
- Artificial anything!
- Anything that contains high fructose corn syrup, so read the label of everything you buy
- If you don't understand what an ingredient is, don't buy it. The fewer ingredients the better. If sugar is one of the first ingredients, don't buy it.
- I won't tell you to avoid caffeinated coffee and tea because I always have a cup in the morning. However, I will tell you to keep it down to one or two cups with nothing fancy in it. Stevia and organic milk if you must.
- Fried and heavily breaded food
- Cookies, cake, pastry, ice cream—you get the idea here
- Dairy, however, if you must have it, please buy organic. You can also try rice, almond, soy, or coconut milk.

- When I dine out, I usually eat vegetarian to avoid any potential processed food. I also talk to the waiter about the food.
- No GMOs (genetically modified food) if possible
- Don't put plastic in the microwave. Actually, don't heat plastic period. I have just about eliminated plastic from our house. I drink my coffee out of a glass bodum and use glass and ceramic as often as possible.
- Wash your hands as often as possible, which is not only just good sense, but it will wash the germs and chemicals off your hands that you'll pick up during the day.

FOODS YOU CAN HAVE

Clean foods. Nothing processed! Choose ONE-ingredient foods (food that doesn't have a label on it).

Plan your meals around food that has NO chemicals in it. If you can't pronounce it, then don't eat it. Of course, this means that you'll probably be cooking at home for most of the week, but that's fine because it's healthier. Make things from scratch. There are dozens of websites, articles, and recipes on "clean eating" that will help you get through the week. I've added two simple recipes at the end of this chapter. (Ron is the chef in our house, not me.)

Foods on the clean-eating list include:

- Fruit, vegetables, and whole grains (preferably organic). Eaten raw is great!
- Lean chicken and fish—organic, grass fed, with no antibiotics or hormones
- LOTS of water (not from the tap please). Add a slice of lemon to help you flush out the toxins.
- Green tea, herbal tea, decaffeinated tea, lemon/ginger-infused water
- Pasta (whole wheat)

- If you eat dairy, go organic.
- Don't eat anything that has been deep fried in oil.
- Try and eat three clean food meals a day with one afternoon snack (and an evening snack for those of you who crave something sweet around nine p.m.)
- Smoothies! (See the back of this chapter for suggestions.)
- Homemade granola
- For snacks, I munch on air-popped popcorn, or I make it the old-fashioned way in a covered pot with oil. There are some *really* nasty chemicals in the microwave popcorn bags, so avoid them. I also eat hummus with carrots and celery, nuts, or fruit for snacks.
- Watch your portion size.
- If it says "fat free" or "natural," put it back. It has other nasty things in it that are unhealthy. Read the label.
- Many clean eaters try to eat five to six small meals a day, instead of three large ones.
- Buy food that is in PBA free cans.
- Avoid plastic and Styrofoam. Use glass or ceramic.

A Typical Day for Me Looks Like This (When I Am Home and Not on the Road)

For breakfast, I'll make a Giambotta Green Smoothie (recipe in the resource section of this book).

For lunch, I make a salad and some cooked vegetables, or I'll often have an organic almond or peanut butter and jelly sandwich. Oatmeal cooked on the stove is also good. I like to add walnuts, raisins, almonds, pumpkin seeds, coconut shavings, and honey. If I go out to lunch, I will eat vegetarian or vegan.

Since I rarely eat red meat and pork, dinner for me is often organic chicken, fish, and vegetables, or a great vegan/vegetarian meal. About twice a year, I'll crave a steak, but it has to be organic from grass-fed cows with no hormones or other chemicals. My plate is mostly vegetables, and they are clean and organic. You can have pasta or a potato, but again, nothing processed.

Snacks are fruit, nuts, air-popped popcorn, toasted garbanzo beans, hummus and carrots or celery, organic yogurt, or homemade granola (really easy to make).

If we want chips, we make them homemade. If my family wants cake, I'll make that from scratch as well. No bagged, boxed, or canned goods.

And, yes, I *love* sweets! So organic ice cream (or a homemade cake or pie) once in a while is pure bliss.

Now for the reality check. Sometimes you are going to slip and eat something you shouldn't. It's fine. Everything in moderation. So don't beat yourself up over it; it's all good.

EXERCISE

I also want you to start walking (if you don't exercise at all) at least three times during the first week for at least thirty minutes for beginners. As the weeks go on, you can walk every other day or every day if you like and up the minutes. You can also swim, jog, or work out at your local gym. It's all good. The main idea here is that you *move*!

I started out by walking for thirty minutes on Tuesday, Thursday, and Saturday. I also used the Couch-to-5K® program (easily found on the Internet) as I like to jog. Whatever works for you is fine.

Any type of movement is acceptable. Walking up the stairs, taking a walk around your neighborhood—it's all good. Please just get off the couch at least once a day.

MIND AND SPIRIT

Every morning you'll be doing my anger and gratitude exercises as well as a few others. This will help retrain your brain into a more positive direction so that you can live a happy life. Happy! What a concept! You *can* be happy now in spite of what is going on around you. Forgive all the layers of your past piece by piece then let it all go. Grace, peace, and love will give you strength; hate, anger, and resentment will make you weak and sick.

At the end of each week, you'll do a review of all that happened. Then you can move on to the next week. As I said before, the worksheets are at the back of this book as well as on my website at www.KatharineGiovanni.com.

CHAPTER THIRTY-FIVE

Our Soles Are the Same

I STARED AT THE COMPUTER, pondering the idea of rainbow moments.

Rainbows and banana peels.

What a life I have led! It's been pure bliss and total hell all the same time.

I think what really started it all was a simple thought I had when I was just a child in elementary school. The thought was a true rainbow moment that changed the course of my life forever.

Here is the story. I think it's a good one to end with.

Have you ever noticed that the soles of our feet are all pretty much the same color?

I have.

I first noticed it when I was a child during gymnastics class. We were all sitting on the floor picking teams for a game. Unfortunately, my best friend and I were the last ones to be picked. So we were on one side, and everyone else was on the other in two groups. As the team leaders were deciding which one of us they would pick, I realized something interesting. Since we were all barefoot at the time, I noticed that the bottom of everyone's feet were all the same color. Although we all looked different physically, everyone had the same basic color on the bottom of their feet.

It's been forty years since that day in gym class, and I still remember it like it was yesterday. That tiny observation changed my life's course because it caused me to look at people in a more healthy way and treat everyone the same. It doesn't matter to me if people are black, white, rich, poor, or even pink with polka dots. People are just people like me, all trying to get through life as best as they can.

We might all be on different roads in life; we might act differently, talk differently, dress differently, and have different beliefs. But at the end of the day, when you get to the bottom of it—the core—our soles are all the same.

CHAPTER THIRTY-SIX

You Have Breast Cancer; Now What Do You Do?

SINCE I AM A BREAST cancer survivor, I wanted to write an open letter to everyone who is going through this horrible disease. My heart and prayers are with you during this hard time. This chapter applies to anyone who is going through an illness.

First and most important, BREATHE.

I can feel your fear and panic through the book.

It's going to be okay.

That being said . . .

The good news is that a breast cancer diagnosis is *not* the death sentence that it used to be. You *can* survive it. I'm living proof.

The most important thing to know right now is this: Your attitude will make or break you. Meaning you need to be positive and *know* that you are going to live.

As I mentioned in a previous chapter of this book, when I was diagnosed, I was sent to chemo class, of all things. As I sat there and listened, the nurse proceeded to tell us all the nasty things that could happen. One side effect after the other and each one worse. As I sat there, my brain snapped, and I mentally decided that I wasn't going to get all those damn side effects. I have no control over the fact that I got cancer, but I sure as hell can control how I get through it. Fast forward, and, no, I never got all those side effects. I was never totally bed ridden. I lost my hair and got really sick, but not as bad as some other people. Why? Because I decided not to. Ninety percent of your happiness and success comes from the inside. So at the end of the day, it's up to you to decide how it will all play out.

After I found the lump, I told my doctor that if my lump was positive for cancer, I wanted an immediate double mastectomy. I didn't want to live with cancer in my body. Good thing I did, as my other breast had cancer cells as well. I had six lymph nodes taken out. The cancer had spread to three but nowhere else, thank God. I was stage 3 triple positive, which means I qualified for Herceptin (breast cancer drug). Since it was an aggressive and fast-growing cancer, my doctor got me into surgery quite fast. Today I am cancer free and intend to stay that way. Since my cancer uses estrogen to grow, I have to be really careful about what I eat.

Here is some good news for you—people survive cancer.

I sat next to a stage 4 cancer survivor who was given only a few months to live—and that was *five* years ago. My advice is to keep your mind positive and try to not stray down the "I'm going to die tomorrow" road.

Listen, at the end of the day, none of us knows how much time we have left. So living each day to the fullest is a gift. I take nothing for granted anymore and will live my life to the fullest with whatever time I have left. There is always a chance that cancer can come back. It's an ugly fact that I have to live with the rest of my life. However, I keep my mind firmly on the fact that I am living to a ripe old age and the cancer chapter is closed.

Here are some tips:

- Listen to your body. When it tells you to rest, you need to rest.
- Increase your protein intake during chemotherapy. *Really* up it. Protein, fruit, and veggies. NO processed foods. You are getting enough poison put into your body so you don't need more. Drink protein shakes.

- Drink *gallons* of water to flush the chemo out of your body. Try to exercise as much as possible. At least walk regularly to keep the blood moving so the chemo can get around your body and kill every single one of those nasty cancer cells.

- Losing hair *is the worst thing*, but it is a small price to pay for life. I suggest that you cut your hair really short before chemo so you can get used to it. Then, when it starts to fall out just shave the darn thing. Forget the crap about cold caps; they don't work. Go out and buy a wig *before* you lose your hair so they can match it to your natural hair color. You can buy some great hat and turbans at http://www.headcovers.com and http://www.tlcdirect.org. Purchase some nice brown eyebrow powder and learn to draw eyebrows. I found some tutorials online that taught me how to do it. It will make you feel better. It made me feel more normal (I hated that skinless cat look). If you want to see what I looked like, go to my website and watch the book trailer for this book.

- Also, ask for pain medication as it will *really* help. Don't fall into the "sleep aid" trap if you have trouble sleeping; those pills are addictive. I bought melatonin at the drug store, and when it got bad, I took a small valium before bed. The doctor wanted to give me antidepression drugs, but I turned them down. I do *not* want to be addicted to that stuff, and I wasn't depressed. I got through it. A valium once in a blue moon is good enough for me.

- Chemo brain is real. You might get a bit forgetful and that's okay. It's temporary.

- Ignore what they tell you about side effects as much as possible. This is *your* journey, and you decide how it will play out. When you do get side effects, breathe your way through and concentrate on the fact that the drug is pushing you toward life.

- Your significant other and family will be in pain, too, and they might need a support group. Although different, their journey through your cancer is just as painful as yours.

Lastly, stay positive. Some days it's easy, and other days it's really hard. It's easy to go into the "I am going to die" mode. Don't die until you are dead.

Stay in life.

Stay for your family.

Stay because you have so much left to give!

Just stay.

CHAPTER THIRTY-SEVEN

The Day that Changed Your Life

SO BEFORE THE BOOK ENDS, let me ask you a question: What if today was the day when your life changed for the better?

If you look back, I'll bet my last dollar that you can remember one day that completely changed your path forever. That one day when your world tilted and it caused you to walk in a new direction.

I have had several days like that over the course of my life. Forks in the road where you have to make a life-changing decision about which road you're going to take. I can remember the first fork in the road I came to. It was a golden rainbow moment.

It was 1979, and I was eighteen years old. I had just graduated from high school and decided to take a year off before I went to college. My dysfunctional childhood had turned me into an angry teenager with no direction. I was tired of being the family ping-pong ball, and I wanted to get away from everyone. So that summer, my father sent me away to a teen Outward Bound program. Mostly to get me out of the hot city, but I think he hoped that it might give me a new perspective on life. Since I had nothing better to do, I agreed and spent the next three months in the woods, hiking up mountains, canoeing down rivers, and generally learning how to survive in nature.

In the middle of the program, we were all required to spend three days alone in the woods. I was given a tent and a small bag of granola, and was placed next to a stream. The counselors checked on me a few times a day but never spoke; they just walked by and waved.

Now, something strange happens to you when you are all alone in the woods—you start to think.

The first thing I did was to hang my food high in a tree so the animals wouldn't get to it. Then I made sure that my tent was set up correctly. I didn't want to get wet if it rained, which, of course, it did later that night.

Then, with nothing left to do, I started to think. I reached for the notebook and pen that I was allowed to bring with me, and I began to write.

My brain took me back, and I examined everything that had happened to me. The memories made me happy, sad, cheerful, and angry. Back and forth, it went as the memories flowed through my mind.

Eventually, the garbage that I had been telling myself (and others) for years and years began to sound really stupid. It's hard to lie to yourself when you are alone with only your thoughts to keep you company.

By the end of the second day, I was finally able to see what I had become, and I didn't like her at all. She was a spoiled and angry brat, who had been given a hard start in life certainly but had a lot going for her in spite of it. I remember sitting under a tree and crying for what seemed like hours. Then once I stopped feeling sorry for myself, I became angry. I stomped around the woods for a while, throwing sticks and rocks and yelling at the air around me.

A few hours later, totally exhausted from expending all that emotion, I found myself on a large boulder by the stream where I had pitched my tent. I can remember watching the sun set behind the mountain. I then stared at the fish in the stream and idly poked at the water with a stick to pass the time. My mind was numb by now, and I felt empty. I had nowhere to go, no one to talk to, and no destination in mind.

It was just about then that it happened. I'm in my fifties now, and I can still remember the exact moment when my entire world changed.

As I looked into the stream, a slow anger started to boil underneath my skin. It was as if something in my brain snapped. I remember thinking about what I was going to do after this solo in the woods, and I decided to show everyone how wrong they were about me. A fierce determination overtook me: I decided right then and there that I would show them all. I would become a lighthouse. I would be an example of how to do it right.

Once the solo was over, I began helping out everywhere I could in camp. I helped build the fires, I carried as much in my pack as I could, and I helped cook every meal. The counselors were stunned and all asked me what brought on the change. They told me that in the years they had been leading kids in the woods, no one had changed as much as I had. I just shrugged and told them that I had simply decided to grow up.

My new path had started.

Unfortunately, it took another fifteen years before I was finally able to become the teacher that I dreamed about on that rock so long ago. Why? Mostly because I was young and had a lot to learn, but I'll never forget the moment when it all started. I'll never forget that sunset and the way the light played with the water in the stream.

As Oprah would say, it was my "ah-ha" moment.

How about you? Can you remember the day that changed your life?

What if today was another one?

What if today you decided to be a lighthouse to the world and change your life?

Why can't we just decide to make today the day? The day when our world changed into a positive, abundant, loving world? The day when we started to do what we actually wanted to do? The day that we started to live our destiny?

The day we decided to be happy.

I think today is a good day to start. A great day to change your world. In fact, let's start with something simple. How about this: The next time you are in line at a drive-through, such as Starbucks, why not pay for the car behind you? Or how about leaving a bigger tip at the next restaurant?

Pass it forward.

Treat people like you want to be treated.

Be a lighthouse and change the world by being an example.

Show everyone how to do it right.

Make today the day that changed your life.

EPILOGUE

IT WAS DONE.

My book was done!

I almost couldn't believe it.

I saved the file and sat back in my chair.

Two years of work done. What a moment, I thought to myself.

I took a deep breath. What a wild ride that was.

As I prepared the file to send to my editor, my mind wandered back to the past. I had been in and out of banana peel fields so many times there were skid marks on my back. You would think after all these years that I would have found a way to anchor myself on those rainbows. I smiled at the thought.

Cancer really was a bridge to a new me. It changed me and opened me up to a brand new life. That was the silver lining here. I woke up from the fog of anger and lack and walked into a life filled with happiness, peace, and love.

Actually, I have had many rainbow and banana peel moments in my life. All have changed me and helped me grow into the person that I am today.

I have no idea what the future brings. I also have no idea when I will stumble into another banana peel field. What I do know is that I now understand that visits in these field are necessary to growth, as uncomfortable as they are. The good news, at least for me, is that I now know how to get out of them when they come along.

After sending the file to Sherry, my editor, I shut the light off to my office and went downstairs.

Katharine 2.0 was here. A new journey had begun.

Katharine's GAAB Life 21-Day Challenge Workbook

THE FOLLOWING PAGES ARE FILLED with worksheets that will help you live a life that goes above and beyond your dreams.

I've included one day's worth of worksheets in this book. For days 2-21, you can either create your own worksheets, answer the questions in a notebook that you keep by your bed, or visit my website at www.KatharineGiovanni.com and download the entire workbook.

I suggest that you try my challenge for one week. Then, if you wish, you can move on to week 2. Slow and steady wins the race here. I think you are going to love how you feel after a week.

I have included a "sample" in front of each worksheet so that you can see how I have filled out my own worksheets. I used to do all of these in a small notebook and often thought it would be great to have worksheets to fill in every day. So I created some.

Log onto my Positive Life Facebook page and let me know how you are doing. Or you can join my GAAB Life 21-Day Challenge Facebook Forum! The links are all on my website at www.katharinegiovanni.com.

YOU CAN DO THIS!

Good luck!

DAY 1: MORNING

Gratitude

First thing in the morning, write down the three greatest things that you are grateful for right now. It doesn't have to be Moses parting the water stuff, it could be that you ate a great slice of pizza. If you want to list more than three, go for it. I usually do this with my first cup of coffee.

For example:
Today I am grateful for:

1. My family
2. My hot cup of coffee
3. My good health

Now it's your turn . . .
Today I am grateful for:

1.
2.
3.

Resentments

Who (or what) do you resent?

Next, write down what you resent right now. You can write names of people, experiences, current circumstance, home, family, or friends. Past or present, anything goes here.

Try and keep the list between one and five. Once you remove these resentments, you can move on to other ones if you have them.

Although I have long since removed these resentments, here are few from when I first did this exercise.

For example:

1. My parent's alcoholism

2. The kids who bullied me in grammar school

3. My father for walking out on us when I was in the eighth grade

Now it's your turn . . .
Who (or what) do you resent?

1.

2.

3.

Now look at the list and seriously think about the **why** for each one. **Why** do you resent this person? Write some thoughts in the space below. Get your emotions out. Use more paper if you need to.

1.

2.

3.

Now release yourself. *Write down their names on the sheet below and* read *each sentence as you do so. You can also forgive situations and resentments. Write up to eight names*

Here's what I do: I take three deep, cleansing breaths and sit quietly and clear my mind. I then write down the people from the resentment section. From there, I write down the first name that comes to my mind. Some days I have eight different names, and other days I write the same name over and over again. It's all correct. One morning I wrote thirty names down. Other days I wrote down situations, places, and groups of people. I also forgave myself. Whatever popped into my head, I immediately wrote it down.

After I'm done, I take another breath and thank God for everything He has done for me.

Forgiveness

Today I can completely and totally forgive the following people for everything, and they completely forgive me. I release all the resentment that I have toward them all.

I completely forgive ________________________________ for all you have done, and you forgive me.

I completely forgive ________________________________ for all you have done, and you forgive me.

I completely forgive ________________________________ for all you have done, and you forgive me.

I completely forgive ________________________________ for all you have done, and you forgive me.

I completely forgive ________________________________ for all you have done, and you forgive me.

I completely forgive ________________________________ for all you have done, and you forgive me.

I completely forgive ________________________________ for all you have done, and you forgive me.

I completely forgive ________________________________ for all you have done, and you forgive me.

Keep going if you wish. There is no limit here.

Write down what you intend to do today. What are you going to accomplish? It can be for business or personal. You can make it really detailed or simple, long or short; it's all good. Here is one of mine:

My ACTION plan for today is:

Finish the project I'm working on in my office

Do some social media marketing—30 minutes

Exercise for 30 minutes

Your turn . . .
My ACTION plan for today is:

DAY 1: EVENING

Tonight before you go to bed, there are a few "end-of-day" worksheets to do. In this worksheet, I would like you to write down what you ate today. Try and keep the food as clean as possible. Again, you can be as detailed as you want.

CLEAN FOOD DIARY for Day 1

	Food Name/Amount
Breakfast	
Snack	
Lunch	
Snack	
Dinner	
Snack	

Next, I would like you to write down what exercise you got today. If you only walked, then write that down. The goal is to do SOME exercise for at least thirty minutes every day.

EXERCISE LOG for Day 1

Type of Activity	Length of Time
Notes:	

Gratitude

Now what are you grateful for tonight? Write as many down as you like. Please write at least three.

Tonight I am grateful for:

1.

2.

3.

What went well today? List at least three positive things that happened to you.

1.

2.

3.

Resentments

Tonight I can completely and totally forgive the following people for everything, and they can completely forgive me. I release all the resentment that I have toward them all.

(Write down the first names that come to mind no matter who they are. You can repeat names from this morning's exercise or write new ones. You can also write down places and experiences if you like.)

I completely forgive ______________________________ for all you have done, and you forgive me.

I completely forgive ______________________________ for all you have done, and you forgive me.

I completely forgive ______________________________ for all you have done, and you forgive me.

I completely forgive ______________________________ for all you have done, and you forgive me.

I completely forgive ______________________________ for all you have done, and you forgive me.

I completely forgive ______________________________ for all you have done, and you forgive me.

I completely forgive ______________________________ for all you have done, and you forgive me.

I completely forgive ______________________________ for all you have done, and you forgive me.

Morning or Nightly Meditation

To end the day, I spend a few minutes sitting on my bed just being. No music, no television, no people. Just me and a silent room. Some call it meditating; others call it prayer. It doesn't matter what you call it. For me personally, this is my time to quietly be with God and the angels for a few minutes.

Sit quietly and close your eyes. You don't have to chant or sit in the lotus position. Just be comfortable.

Now concentrate on your breath. Watch it go in and then out again. Pay close attention to your breathing. Center your mind on it. This will quiet your brain.

As the minutes go on, you might pay attention to the thoughts or images that float into your brain. As they come into your awareness, allow them to float out again. Sometimes I'll do this with a pad of paper and a pen nearby so that I can write down what comes to my mind. Other times I will just be.

Keep focusing for about five minutes and then quietly open your eyes.

(There are some great apps that can help you with this. I recently discovered Headspace, an app for my iPhone and a great beginner's tool.)

If you wish to download the entire Katharine's GAAB Life 21-Day Challenge Workbook, please visit www.KatharineGiovanni.com.

Resources

RECIPES

Katharine's Giambotta Smoothie

Giambotta is traditionally an Italian stew. However, my mother-in-law used the name as a catch-all for "anything I have in the refrigerator mixed with eggs." So in honor of Eleanor, I've named my breakfast smoothie the Giambotta Smoothie. Why? Because it's literally anything we have in the vegetable crisper mixed with spinach and coconut milk.

Everyone *knows* they need to eat more fruit and vegetables, but who has the time to cook it all the time? That's why it's faster (for me at least) to drink the fruits/veggies in the morning and get it over with.

I also suggest that you research what fruits and vegetables you should be eating to help with whatever is ailing you. Since I'm a breast cancer *thriver,* I concentrate on dark green veggies, cruciferous vegetables, and fruit.

We use a blender (Ninja Blender) because we like the pulp and want the fiber and vitamins. I always drink the smoothie in the morning before I've eaten anything, usually right after my work out on the treadmill.

The ingredients are about 40 percent greens and 60 percent fruit. This recipe makes enough for two to drink for breakfast. The fruit is what makes this a meal as it will fill you up. Some people even add oats and/or yogurt to it. The trick to adding oats is to grind the oats into a fine powder and then add in to the mixture.

Here's the basic recipe. Sometimes I'll put all these ingredients in;

sometimes I won't. It really depends on what we have in our refrigerator. Spinach, apple, banana, turmeric, and ginger are always in it.

1 or 2 cups organic spinach (amount depends on how many people you are making this for)
1 tablespoon ginger or freshly ground ginger root
1 tablespoon tumeric or freshly ground turmeric root. I prefer using the root which is available in many grocery stores as well as Whole Foods.
1 or 2 cups additional dark green leafy vegetables such as kale, bok choy, parsley, broccoli, cabbage, lettuce, or chard—the darker the leaf the better. Switch up your greens.
2 to 4 pieces of fruit such as apple, banana, or berries, whatever you have on hand
¼ cup fresh raw beet
¼ cup cucumber
¼ cup carrot
One celery stick
Lemon
Coconut milk (or orange juice)
You can also use filtered water if you like
Sometimes I'll add Greek yogurt

When we first started this, Ron started to lose weight and I started to *gain* weight. Argh! After gaining a few pounds, I searched the Internet and discovered that I shouldn't be using orange juice. Rookie mistake. I immediately switched the orange juice to unsweetened coconut milk.

Now, I know how busy you are. So here's what I do: Every Sunday I purchase all my fruit and vegetables. I'll then get out seven freezer bags and divide everything up into seven portions. I will then toss a few bags in the freezer and a few in the fridge. Now whenever I want to make a Giambotta Smoothie, all I have to do is grab a bag, add coconut milk and a little water, and drink. I'll often change up my smoothie packs and put different fruit and greens in them to keep things interesting. If you are not always the one making the smoothies, you might want to label each bag and include what liquid to add to it.

By the way, the freezer method will make your smoothie thick, like a milkshake. If you want it thinner, then you can keep your bags in the fridge. Just make a few bags at a time so the greens and fruit don't spoil.

I hope you enjoy it.

Homemade Granola

One cup of each of the following:

Rolled oats
Steel cut oats (if you wish)
Raisins
Walnuts
Almonds
Sunflower seeds (½ cup)
Pumpkin seeds
Coconut shavings
2–3 tablespoons olive oil
1 teaspoon vanilla
½ teaspoon nutmeg
1 tablespoon cinnamon

Butter a cookie sheet so the mixture doesn't stick. Bake at 325 degrees for 20 minutes. Then take a look and stir it around. Bake for another 10 minutes. Stir again. Maybe five more. Bake until brown. (I burned the first batch.)

Serve with honey or maple syrup (if you have a sweet tooth) and milk. You can also mix it with vanilla yogurt (organic, of course) and fresh fruit.

BIBLIOGRAPHY

ABC News. "21 Easy Ways to Eat Fruits and Veggies Every Day." http://abcnews.go.com/Health/22-easy-ways-eat-fruits-veggies-day/story?id=23410924&ts=true#5.

Achor, Shawn. *The Happiness Advantage: The Seven Principles of Positive Psychology that Fuel Success and Performance at Work*. New York: Crown Business.

Blum, Deborah. "The Plunge of Pleasure: Like All Roller-Coaster Rides, Dopamine Highs Have Their Dangers." *Psychology Today*. http://www.psychologytoday.com/articles/200909/the-plunge-pleasure.

Brown, Harriet. "How to Forgive Anyone—and Why Your Health Depends on It." http://www.oprah.com/oprahs-lifeclass/How-to-Forgive-Others-Health-Benefits-of-Forgiveness-Fred-Luskin#ixzz3ORMWJ7MI.

Crazy Sexy Cancer. http://kriscarr.com/products/crazy-sexy-cancer/.

Food Matters. http://www.foodmatters.tv/.

Forks Over Knives. http://www.forksoverknives.com/.

Hudson, Clare. "5-Step Forgiveness Meditation Exercise." http://thoughtbrick.com/meditation/5-step-forgiveness-meditation-exercise/.

Huffington, Arianna. On Becoming Fearless. http://www.mentorschannel.com/AriannaHuffington/OnBecomingFearless.

Montier, James. "Global Equity Strategy: The Psychology of Happiness." http://www.trendfollowing.com/whitepaper/happiness.pdf.

Sisterhood of the Shrinking Jeans. "Top 10 Tips for Eating Clean." http://shrinkingjeans.net/2013/05/top-10-tips-for-eating-clean/.

Skinny Ms. "10 Clean Eating Tips: Do's and Dont's." http://skinnyms.com/10-clean-eating-tips-dos-and-donts/.

Super Juice Me. http://www.superjuiceme.com/.

The Forgiveness Experiment. hhttp://forgiveness.healingjourney.biz/forgiveness%20exp_004.htm.

The Gracious Pantry. http://www.thegraciouspantry.com/clean-eating/.

The Healthy Apple. "What Is Clean Eating?" http://thehealthyapple.com/what-is-clean-eating/.

Tiny Buddha. "How to Forgive Someone When It's Hard: 30 Tips to Let Go of Anger." http://tinybuddha.com/blog/how-to-forgive-someone-when-its-hard-30-tips-to-let-go-of-anger/.

Vanzant, Iyanla. "3 Tools To Help You Forgive Someone." http://www.healyourlife.com/author-iyanla-vanzant/2013/12/wisdom/inspiration/3-ways-to-forgive.

Vanzant, Iyanla. "The Power of Forgiveness." http://live.huffingtonpost.com/r/segment/iyanla-vanzant-on-the-power-of-forgiveness/52b21cee2b8c2a24d1000284.

Voogd, Peter. "What It Takes to Go From Dead Broke to 6 Figures in 6 Months." *Entrepreneur*. http://www.entrepreneur.com/article/240510.

Women's Health. "Q&A: Do You Have to Give Up Meat if You Want to Eat Clean?" http://www.womenshealthmag.com/nutrition/clean-eating.

ACKNOWLEDGMENTS

SO MANY PEOPLE HAVE HELPED me become a cancer survivor! Although there are too many to name, I would like to mention a few special people . . .

First and most important, my incredible husband and sons: Ron, Matt, and Jeremy Giovanni.

I would also like to thank my outstanding medical team including Dr. Ndidi Azikiwe, MD; Dr. Karl W. Schwarz, MD; Dr. Neeraj R. Agrawal, MD; Melissa Smith, PA; and Dr. John Riley. Thanks are not enough. Words are not enough. You are all earth angels.

Special thanks also goes to my outstanding editor, Sherry Roberts; Harmonie Ponder, who designed the cover; and Nancy Jo Photography for taking such a great headshot.

My most sincere thanks also goes out to all my friends and family from around the country. Without you all I would have crashed on the rocks years ago!

KATHARINE GIOVANNI IS A TWO-TIME award-winning author, international speaker, and the world's leading concierge trainer and consultant. She is considered to be one of the founders of the independent concierge industry and is the most sought-after concierge consultant and trainer in the world.

A proud breast cancer survivor, Katharine is a dynamic speaker who offers high content with a motivational/inspirational style. She has appeared at seminars and conferences around the world teaching workshops to groups, individuals, and corporations.

Katharine is the author of four books including her two-time award-winning book *Going Above and Beyond*, and her acclaimed book *The Concierge Manual.*

Katharine's thirty-year career started in 1984 in New York City where she was a receptionist for an advertising agency. In 1986, she started her event planning career and went on to become an event planner and concierge for Fortune 500 executives. She started her first company in 1995.

In 1998, a handful of pioneers discovered the world of the independent concierge, and Katharine was one of them. If you looked around the US back then, you might have found two dozen concierge services, but certainly no more than that. Sensing a need, Katharine propelled her meeting planning business into something more cutting edge: a company that offered concierge services to an eclectic range of industries that had yet to discover the world of the concierge.

In 2000, she founded the International Concierge and Lifestyle Management Association (ICLMA), one of the first associations for the concierge industry, and in 2014, Katharine successfully transitioned ICLMA into the extremely popular ICLM Directory.

Katharine has been interviewed by dozens of publications and appeared on radio and television shows around the country including *ABC News Nightline*, *CBS News*, *Good Morning America*, MTV, *Time Magazine*, *Money Magazine*, *Forbes*, *The New York Times*, and *The Wall Street Journal*, to name a few.

Katharine was raised in New York City, earned a BA from Lake Forest College, and currently lives in North Carolina.

For more information about Katharine, please visit her websites at www.KatharineGiovanni.com and www.TriangleInternational.com